THE DIESEL ⚡ BROTHERS

A TRUCKING AWESOME GUIDE TO TRUCKS AND LIFE

HEAVY D &
DIESEL DAVE

GALLERY BOOKS

NEW YORK   LONDON   TORONTO   SYDNEY   NEW DELHI

Gallery Books
An Imprint of Simon & Schuster, Inc.
1230 Avenue of the Americas
New York, NY 10020

First Gallery Books trade paperback edition September 2020

GALLERY BOOKS and colophon are trademarks of Simon & Schuster, Inc.

For information about special discounts for bulk purchases, please contact Simon & Schuster Special Sales at 1-866-506-1949 or business@simonandschuster.com.

The Simon & Schuster Speakers Bureau can bring authors to your live event. For more information, or to book an event, contact the Simon & Schuster Speakers Bureau at 1-866-248-3049 or visit our website at www.simonspeakers.com.

Interior design by Jaime Putorti

Manufactured in the United States of America

10 9 8 7 6 5 4 3 2 1

Library of Congress Cataloging-in-Publication Data is available.

ISBN 978-1-5011-7315-8
ISBN 978-1-9821-6959-6 (pbk)
ISBN 978-1-5011-7317-2 (ebook)

A special thanks to our parents, who raised us right; our spouses and children, who love us, support us, and push us to be the best we can be; and of course to the Diesel Gods, who have blessed us with the ability and the opportunity to show the world the wonders of Diesel!

To God, our family, and our friends: Thank you! Life has been an awesome ride, and we have made some great memories and can't wait for the stories we will be able to tell from the adventures that are yet to come!

Dave and Dave
Diesel Brothers

CONTENTS

INTRODUCTION
THE ROAD SO FAR

HEAVY D: Hey, ladies and gentlemen, this is Dave Sparks, and you guys might know me as Heavy D from the Discovery Channel show *Diesel Brothers*. In the world of diesel trucks, no one has more fun or builds bigger or more badass trucks than me and my best friend, Diesel Dave, and our hardworking crew in Salt Lake City. Our business model is pretty simple: we buy another man's junk—beat-up, wrecked, or broken-down trucks—and transform them into extreme and tricked-out treasures.

> Our business model is pretty simple: we buy another man's junk—beat-up, wrecked, or broken-down trucks—and transform them into extreme and tricked-out treasures.

Sometimes we turn the trucks for a pretty sweet profit, but about six times a year, we give them away to very lucky fans.

Now, you're probably sitting there thinking: *Who in the world gives away free trucks? Have you guys lost your minds? Have you inhaled too much exhaust?* I know the concept might sound crazy. It's kind of just how we roll.

Hey, believe me: it has been a wild ride for us to get this far, with plenty of road bumps, potholes, and speed traps along the way. Just a few years ago, we were a couple of young entrepreneurs with big dreams simply trying to pay our bills and get our feet under us. But then our builds started becoming popular with diesel truck enthusiasts on social media, and people inquired about how to buy them or have one built of their own. So we thought giving away one of our monster builds in a contest would be a great way to drum up interest and generate publicity for our companies.

Well, the first sweepstakes went so well we started doing a handful every year. And the amazing thing about our giveaways is that you only have to buy a T-shirt or something else off our website to enter. Even better: most of the people who have won our trucks were really in need and could use them. Believe me, there's nothing better than seeing people screaming, crying, and jumping for joy when they find out they've won. It's really cool—it's like being Santa Claus in real life.

> Believe me, there's nothing better than seeing people screaming, crying, and jumping for joy when they find out they've won. It's really cool—it's like being Santa Claus in real life.

And it's not like we're giving away our grandpa's farm truck, either. Our trucks are one of a kind, unlike anything else out there. We break the conventional rules of truck repair and build trucks the way we want to do them—often creating rides that no one thought was possible. We turn short beds into long beds, four doors into six doors, crew cabs into mega-cabs, and gassers into diesels. We enhance, rebuild, or replace engines and transmissions to create crazy horsepower and torque, but our work only begins under the hood. We trick out trucks with new lifts, bumpers, fender flares, lights, custom paint, wheels, and tires to turn them into sleek, unforgettable machines.

In every one of our projects, we want to build a truck that looks good, but we also want it to function. We build every truck to be worked and used; these aren't show trucks. Our trucks have to be dependable and rugged because the people buying them (or winning them) are going to depend on them and push them to the limits, whether it's on the highway to work or in the desert or mountains on the weekend. That's why we thoroughly test every truck we build—and that's when the real fun usually begins!

In the pages that follow, you'll learn more about our story and lives from before *Diesel Brothers* and after! Hey, fasten your seat belt. We're only getting started and it has been one hell of a ride so far!

DIESEL DAVE: Howdy, folks, this is Dave Kiley, otherwise known as Diesel Dave. If you didn't know already, Heavy D and

I aren't really brothers. In fact, we're not related at all. But the man is definitely my brother from another mother, and we're about as close to blood relatives as you can get because both of us have diesel running through our veins. We're best friends, we've lived together, we work together, worship together, and do just about everything else together. As our wives like to say, we put the "bro" in bromance.

> *We're best friends, we've lived together, we work together, worship together, and do just about everything else together. As our wives like to say, we put the "bro" in bromance.*

When Heavy D asked me to come on board and help him build his used car company a few years ago, I couldn't resist. He's one of the most determined people I know, and I knew he was going to be successful at anything he did. Of course, I had no idea then that we'd be building legendary diesel trucks. I know one thing: it's a heck of a lot better than buying and selling Hyundais and Volvo station wagons. I've always loved driving and working on diesel trucks. They're so much fun to drive and chicks absolutely dig them! Joe Diffie told us in a song that trucks are meant for guys to get girls and for guys to impress girls. Chicks dig the long ball and big trucks, no question about it.

> *Chicks dig the long ball and big trucks, no question about it.*

While we're obviously known for our killer trucks, I think people watch *Diesel Brothers* because we have so much fun together. You never know what's going to happen in our garage—we might be pulling pranks on each other or a truck might even catch on fire! There's always something crazy happening. If you've watched our show, you know that we have a wicked sense of humor and no one is immune from our practical jokes. We like to make fun of each other and laugh with each other. We're constantly trying to come up with new pranks and ways to get even with the other guys in our shop.

Practical jokes are really what made us so popular on social media, and then Jay Leno noticed one of our YouTube videos, in which I "rolled coal" on one of our buddies while he was using the restroom. (Don't try this at home, but that's when you hook an irrigation pipe up to a truck's tailpipe and blow exhaust on your friend!) My appearance on *The Tonight Show* with Leno led to a bunch of TV producers calling and wanting us to do a reality TV show. To be honest, we really weren't too keen on having camera crews following us around every day. We weren't too interested in becoming the next *Keeping Up with the Kardashians* or *Real Housewives of New Jersey*.

Like I said earlier, Heavy D and I are best friends, and everybody in our garage gets along with everyone else, and we wanted to keep it that way. We didn't want to ruin our chemistry in the garage. Besides, when a producer called us about taping an audition tape for Discovery Channel, we thought he was like one of those guys in Dubai who emails you and asks for ten thousand dollars. We couldn't figure out why he'd want to put us on TV. But he ended up being a guy we could trust, and the next thing you knew, we had a TV show.

Diesel Brothers really hasn't changed us much. Having a TV show is an unbelievable opportunity for us to spread diesel joy to everyone around the world, and we know it won't last forever. But, as long as we're doing it, we're going to put the pedal to the floor and enjoy the ride.

DIESEL HANDBOOK LESSON NO. 1
DIESEL OR GASOLINE?

It's probably the question I get asked more than any other: Why should I buy a truck with a diesel engine instead of one with a gasoline engine? To be honest, it really depends on what you want to do with your truck.

If you're looking for an everyday driver, a truck you can drive to and from work and to your kids' baseball and soccer games on the weekends, then you'll probably want a gasoline engine. If you're driving in town and want some off-the-line acceleration and immediate power when you put the pedal to the floor, a gas engine is probably for you.

On the other hand, if you're going to use your truck to pull a boat to the lake or camper into the mountains, or if you're going to be hauling a trailer with lawn maintenance equipment and other heavy loads, you'll probably want a diesel engine. While gasoline engines are known for their horsepower, diesel engines produce torque, which is perfect for hauling heavy loads up steep grades and for long distances.

Think of it this way: A truck with a gasoline engine is a sleek, chiseled racehorse like Secretariat. It's going to be fast out of the gates and one hell of a sprinter. On the other hand, a truck with a diesel engine is going to be like the Budweiser

Clydesdales. It's not going to be quite as fast off the line, but it's going to be strong and powerful as an ox.

Compared to gasoline engines, diesel engines are simpler, more efficient, and more economical. In other words, diesel engines use less fuel, they're easier to fix, and they're going to last a heck of a lot longer than gasoline engines. Diesel engines are also safer, because diesel fuel is far less volatile and its vapor is far less explosive than gasoline. On average, diesel engines get between 10 to 15 miles per gallon more than their gasoline counterparts, and some diesel engines have lasted as long as 900,000 miles!

Now, I know you probably didn't buy this book for a history lesson, but here it goes: The diesel engine has been around since the late nineteenth century, but for whatever reason, it has never really caught on in the United States. Gasoline engines have been far more popular in American cars and trucks, even though the diesel engine is much more efficient and durable. Fortunately, that trend is starting to change and diesel engines are becoming more common.

Rudolf Diesel, a German engineer, invented the diesel engine in 1892. He was inspired to invent the diesel engine because gasoline engines were so inefficient. At the time, only about 10 percent of the fuel in gasoline engines was being used to actually move vehicles; the rest was being released through useless heat out the tailpipe! Talk about waste! Diesel wanted to create an engine with much higher efficiency.

Like gasoline engines, a diesel engine is a type of internal combustion engine, which is designed to convert chemical energy into mechanical energy. Fuel is burned inside the main part of the engine (the cylinders), where power is produced, and the mechanical energy moves pistons up and down inside the cylinders, and the pistons are connected to a crankshaft, which creates the rotary motion needed to turn wheels. Do you follow me?

Internal combustion engines are more efficient than external combustion engines like steam engines because everything happens in the same place. Once heat is produced, it doesn't have to flow somewhere else to make pistons (and wheels) move.

Even though gasoline and diesel engines both work by internal combustion, they function in slightly different ways. In gasoline engines, fuel and air are injected into the cylinders. A piston compresses the mixture and makes it explosive, and a small electric spark from a spark plug ignites it. That makes the mixture explode, which generates power to push the piston down the cylinder and then through the crankshaft and gears to turn the wheels. Voilà! You have a moving vehicle!

In diesel engines, air is compressed into far less space, making it much hotter than the air used in gasoline engines. In fact, the air is so hot—usually about 1,000 degrees Fahrenheit—that a spark plug isn't even needed to ignite the mixture of air and fuel. Instead, once the air is compressed, a mist of fuel sprayed into the cylinder by injectors automatically ignites to create energy. The best news: a diesel engine doesn't need a routine ignition tune-up because it doesn't have spark plugs and distributors!

In summary, diesel engines use far less fuel than their gasser counterparts, diesel fuel generally costs the same as gasoline and is much more energy dense, and diesel cars and trucks require far less maintenance. While most gasoline vehicles recommend oil changes every 3,000 miles, service intervals for diesel engines can reach as far as every 10,000 miles. A diesel truck or car might cost you more in the beginning, but it's going to save you a boatload of cash in fuel efficiency and maintenance over the life of the vehicle.

–Heavy D

CHAPTER ONE
HEAVY D

HEAVY D: My friends and family members have been calling me "Heavy D" since high school, when I first used the nickname as a joke. (No, I wasn't some wannabe rapper.) For whatever reason, the moniker kind of stuck with me. I actually came into this world as David William Sparks on January 5, 1985. To be honest, my life was heavy from the time I took my first breath. I was born in Cumberland, Maryland, not far from Walter Reed National Military Medical Center, where my father, Bill Sparks, was battling an inoperable brain tumor.

When I was about a month old, doctors told my twenty-seven-year-old father that he had only two years left to live. They told him there wasn't anything else they could do for him medically, that chemotherapy and radiation weren't working to reduce the size of his tumor, and that it was probably best if he went home and spent what little time he had left with his family.

So he and my mom, Lisa, loaded up us kids and returned to Layton, Utah, on the eastern edge of the Great Salt Lake, which is near where my maternal grandparents lived. I was the youngest of their four children. My sisters, Michelle and Alicia, and brother, Taylor, were older than me, but all of us were too young to understand what was happening to my dad.

As my father prepared for the final months of his life, he and my mom decided to make videotaped messages from him, which she planned to show us when we were older. In many ways, my father wanted to use those recordings to introduce himself to us, so we would never forget him when he was gone. My dad was born and raised in Topeka, Kansas, but moved to Southern California when he was in high school. He loved to surf in the Pacific Ocean and always wanted to be doing something outdoors. I think that's where I get my passion for extreme sports and being outside.

He told us about what we should and shouldn't do, how to treat others, and other virtues he would have shared with us if he'd lived long enough to be our dad.

In those video recordings, my dad shared important lessons he believed he'd never get a chance to teach us. He told us about what we should and shouldn't do, how to treat others, and other virtues he would have shared with us if he'd lived long enough to be our dad.

More than anything else, he taught us about being selfless,

living our lives for others, and about our duty to share the gospel with others.

When my dad was fifteen years old, he converted to Christianity and joined the Church of Jesus Christ of Latter-day Saints. He went on a two-year mission trip to Zurich, Switzerland, and Munich, Germany, which is where he met my mom, who was born into the LDS church. They fell in love and were engaged—after only two real dates—under a lifeguard stand in Huntington Beach, California. Shortly after they married at the Mormon temple in Ogden, Utah, in August 1979, my dad unexpectedly lost his job. He couldn't find another one, so he joined the Army National Guard. While my dad was stationed at boot camp in Alabama, he suffered a seizure and doctors diagnosed him with a malignant, inoperable brain tumor.

Once we returned to Utah, my father's condition worsened. He had to take methadone and morphine to survive debilitating headaches as the tumor grew. Then a truly amazing thing happened. When doctors told my dad he had only three weeks to live, he received a priesthood blessing from our church. Our former mission director told my dad that he would live long enough to see his children grow up. During the next few weeks, my father became stronger and stronger. He was still in quite a bit of pain, but the blessing gave him hope to continue living.

Then my dad received another blessing from our home teacher in the church, who told him he would be healed because of the faith of his children. My dad was so convinced the tumor would go away that he stopped taking his pain medica-

Six months later, the tumor was undetectable on brain scans. His doctors called it spontaneous remission, but we knew it was a miracle and answer to our prayers.

tion. Six months later, the tumor was undetectable on brain scans. His doctors called it spontaneous remission, but we knew it was a miracle and answer to our prayers.

If that doesn't make you believe in the Almighty, I guess nothing will.

My dad continued to suffer seizures and his cancer treatments had left him with short-term memory loss, so he was unable to take a full-time job. His hobby was restoring Volkswagen buses—the kind you used to see at Grateful Dead concerts in the 1960s—and old motorcycles in our garage. He made money by installing car stereos in our driveway. That's probably where I first learned about tearing things apart and then putting them back together. Amazingly, my dad went back to college when he was forty and earned a bachelor of science degree in manufacturing engineering from Weber State University in 1997. What he lacked in memory, he made up for in personality and determination. His professors loved him and appreciated his hard work. He graduated with a 3.0 grade-point average, despite his health problems.

When my dad was sick, my mom went to work to keep a roof over our heads and make sure we were fed. She had a bachelor's degree in elementary education, but she wanted to stay home with us kids. She was the master of part-time jobs, selling pizzas at special events and babysitting for families in our neighborhood. She sewed for a children's clothing store and even made some of our clothes by hand. She taught us about hard work. One summer, my brother, my sisters, and I delivered enough handbills to earn enough money to go to Disneyland. While we might not have had much in material possessions, we knew we were blessed because we were together and my dad was still with us.

Some of my favorite memories of my childhood occurred at my grandfather's farm. When I was only six years old, I drove his Ford tractor and plowed a quarter acre of land over and over again. By the time I was finished, his farm resembled the Dust Bowl! With my dad teaching me about motorcycles and VW buses, and my grandfather teaching me about heavy equipment, I became fascinated with anything that had an engine and wheels. Because of their influence, I was a gearhead from the start.

When I was eleven, my brother and I saved $80 and bought a 1976 Yamaha YZ80 dirt bike, which was the first motorized vehicle I owned. Unfortunately, we spent most of our time— and what little money we had left—replacing the plastic clutch and gearshift levers, which seemed to break every other time Taylor rode it. Eventually, I bought my brother out and the dirt bike was my toy. I spent all of my time riding it and working on it. While my other buddies were playing baseball, basket-ball, football, and other team sports, I only wanted to ride my dirt bike. To be honest, I was more interested in a sport that required having more than one ball.

When I was a little bit older, I sold the YZ80 and bought my cousin's Suzuki RM250. It was really way too big for me and my feet couldn't even hit the ground when I was riding it. I had to stand on a milk carton to climb onto the seat, but I rode that dirt bike about every day and grew into it.

With those two bikes, I learned valuable early lessons about properly maintaining your vehicle—regular maintenance is the key to reliability; irregular maintenance is the key to great exercise.

With those two bikes, I learned valuable early lessons about properly maintaining your vehicle—regular maintenance is the key to reliability; irregular maintenance is the key to great exercise.

Believe me, I found out quickly that motocross boots aren't made for walking. I learned to make sure the bike's oil was changed on time, its chain was oiled, clean, and tight, and the air pressure in its tires was right.

By the time I was in middle school, I was already taking shop classes, where I learned to weld and work on engines. I built a skateboard ramp and welded a metal rail to it. My buddies and I shredded the thing out. At Layton High School, probably half of my classes focused on either automotive mechanics, fabrication, or welding. By the time I was a senior, I was seriously interested in becoming an auto mechanic. Hey, when you're constantly washing your hands *before* you use the restroom, that's probably a good sign that you might have a future in working on cars and trucks.

Hey, when you're constantly washing your hands before you use the restroom, that's probably a good sign that you might have a future in working on cars and trucks.

Shortly after I was old enough to get my driver's license, my grandfather gave me a $1,500 loan to purchase a 1993 Jeep Cherokee. I was already working by then, helping my grandfather and uncle, John Tanner, build houses. He knew I'd pay him back. About a month after I bought the blue Jeep Cherokee, the water pump went out. I told my mom I needed to find someone to fix it, but she told me we didn't have the money to get it repaired.

Instead, she drove me to an auto parts store, bought a water pump, and left me alone in our garage to fix it. When I complained to her that I didn't know how to replace it, she told me to figure it out. My mom was great about telling me I could do things I didn't think I could do. She encouraged me to test my limits and learn new things. Changing that water pump was my first real-life experience working on a vehicle. It took me a few tries to get it right with my dad's prized Snap-on tools, but I eventually replaced the water pump, and the Jeep was up and running again.

Unfortunately, a few weeks later, I flipped my Jeep Cherokee while racing a buddy in an unfinished neighborhood near our house. The curbs in the subdivision were really high, and they hadn't yet poured asphalt on the road, and I underestimated a wide turn. The Jeep flipped on its side, smashing in the passenger's side and shattering the window in the back door. I told my parents I'd rolled it over in a ditch. I couldn't afford to replace the window—and I didn't know anything about bodywork yet—so I drove a smashed-up Jeep Cherokee (with plastic on the window) to school for the rest of the year. After I saved some money, I found a replacement window at a salvage yard and sold the Jeep that summer.

Even back then, I didn't hang on to my vehicles for very long. It seems like I've always had attention deficit disorder when it comes to cars. For whatever reason, I quickly lose interest in driving them and I always seem to be looking for the next great thing. The Jeep Cherokee was my first experience flipping a vehicle—both literally and figuratively—and I ended up selling it for $3,000, which was twice as much as what I paid for it. I used the money to buy a full-sized 1988 Chevrolet Blazer, which is where I first learned about big power and really modifying trucks. I put a lift on it, along with bigger and better wheels and tires, and added straight-pipe exhaust, which made it sound louder and a hell of a lot meaner. I graduated from high school in 2003 and sold the Chevy Blazer right before I left the country for my two-year LDS mission.

Growing up in the Church of Jesus Christ of Latter-day Saints, and after hearing my parents talk about their mission trips for most of my life, I thought it would be a cool experience and an important thing to do. My parents liked to talk to each other in German when I was growing up, and none of us kids could understand what they were saying. I thought going to a foreign place, learning the native language, and adapting to a new culture would be a valuable life lesson for me. Of course, it meant I would have to spend two years away from my parents, which wasn't going to be easy for them or me, especially being away from my dad for so long. We didn't know how much time he had left.

Miraculously, my father lived twenty-two years after doctors told him he had only months to live in 1985. Despite his health struggles, he never gave up and he enjoyed life to the fullest. The elders in our church were right: he lived long enough to see his kids grow up. No matter the hand my dad was dealt, he kept going and going. That's why we affectionately called him the "Energizer Bunny." He died on May 22, 2007, about a year after I returned from my mission trip. He was forty-nine years old. When the brain tumors returned, he fought cancer valiantly until the very end. My dad taught me more about courage and overcoming adversity than anyone I've ever known, and his life is truly a testament to God's strength and renewal.

> My dad taught me more about courage and overcoming adversity than anyone I've ever known, and his life is truly a testament to God's strength and renewal.

My father's death really took a toll on my family, especially my mother, after we'd seen him fight for so long. But we know our family will be together again. After spending much of her life as a homemaker, my mom took a job working as a gate agent for an airline and she was later hired as a flight attendant. She has traveled all over the world, to places such as China, India, and Peru, helping the impoverished and continuing her mission work. Her job also allows her to spend considerable time with her thirteen grandchildren, who are scattered across the country. She keeps herself busy—she even works part-time filling retail orders in our warehouse—and looks for opportunities to serve others. It's another one of the lessons my father taught each of us.

CHAPTER TWO
DIESEL DAVE

DIESEL DAVE: I bounced around all over the place as a kid, which might explain the reason for my nomadic existence and restlessness as a young adult. I was born on June 17, 1984, which makes me about six months older—and a heck of a lot wiser—than Heavy D. Unlike him, though, I didn't earn my moniker, "Diesel Dave," until much later in life, and I'll share those details with you later in the book.

I was born in Lubbock, Texas, where my dad, Mike Kiley, was stationed at Reese Air Force Base. He was in pilot training, with fifty-four other students. The top 10 percent of students got their choice of planes. Dad wanted an F-15 fighter, and his performance up to that point told him he would probably get it. Then I tried to enter the world two months early, and Mom went on bed rest. Dad apparently dropped just below the top

10 percent and was slotted as an instructor in the T-37, which was a twin-engine Cessna the air force used for decades to train its pilots. We spent four more years in Lubbock, and that's okay because my sister Kerstin was born there, too, and so there are two of us Texans in the family.

I had my first set of stitches while living on Yount Street at Reese Air Force Base. I was hanging out in the front yard, and I must have been about three years old at the time. I'd discovered that if you threw a big rock as hard as you could onto the ground, it would break open, and the insides of rocks are sometimes really cool to look at. I was busy smashing rocks when my older sister, Amber, came out and said, "Come on, David, Mom's taking us to McDonald's." Well, I had one more rock to smash. It was the biggest one yet. I picked it up and swung it back, but in all the excitement I forgot to let go. The rock continued backward in my hands until it slammed into the back of my head and split my head open.

The emergency room staff had a tough time buying the story. But with Amber reminding me over and over how I ruined her trip to McDonald's, they stitched me up and let us get on with our day.

When I was four years old, Dad was assigned to fly the KC-135Q, a big Boeing aerial refueling plane, and we moved to Beale Air Force Base, outside Wheatland, California. The Q model was designed to refuel the SR-71 spy plane, also called the Blackbird.

We lived on the base for a while; I liked it there. We'd go

back into the streams and creeks behind our house and catch crawdads and build forts in the woods. We didn't stay on the base long, though; my folks decided to buy a house in Sacramento, California. Right before my dad's commitment to the air force was set to expire, Operation Desert Storm came to a peak, and my dad went to war. He refueled everything that flew, flying back and forth like a gas station in the sky. My dad was a bona fide American hero, at least in my eyes. I was almost eight when Dad came back from the war. We sold our house, Dad left the air force, and we moved to Kaysville, Utah. He was hired as a commercial airline pilot for Delta Air Lines in 1991 and still flies for the airline today.

Growing up in the Kiley house was quite an adventure. There were seven of us kids. My mom, Kellee, could have been anything she wanted to be, but she chose to be our mom and a homemaker. There wasn't anything my mom didn't know how to do. She was a doctor, a teacher, a psychologist, a cabdriver, a repairman, and a zillion other things.

There wasn't anything my mom didn't know how to do. She was a doctor, a teacher, a psychologist, a cabdriver, a repairman, and a zillion other things.

She coached my baseball Little League team and taught me how to tie a dozen different knots when I was a Cub Scout. My folks taught us to work hard and to serve others. I was the second-oldest kid and oldest boy, right behind my older sister, Amber, and ahead of my younger sisters, Kerstin, Jenny, and Grace, and younger brothers, Joseph and Keith. It was so much fun growing up in a big family, there was never a dull moment, and I always had someone to hang out with and find trouble with.

After a couple of years in Kaysville, my parents bought a bigger house in Farmington, Utah, which provided us with even more adventures on a much larger and spectacular playground. Our new house was at the foothills of the Wasatch Mountains, where we liked to hike and ride our bikes. Then we were spoiled some more when my dad bought us a four-wheeler. We rode it up and down the mountain trails until Amber and her friend Sara rolled it. Fortunately, no one was seriously hurt, but I'm not going to lie: it took me a while to forgive her for that.

My sisters and I had some great times together. I remember going to Lagoon, a large amusement park right in Farmington. All of us wanted to ride the giant Ferris wheel. When we got to the ride, we found there were too many of us to fit in one bucket, so we divided up. My mom and her friend took the younger children; my sisters Amber, Kerstin, and Jenny and our friend Chelsea and me went in another bucket. The buckets weren't next to each other. In fact, they were as far apart as possible. When ours was on the top of the wheel, theirs was at the bottom. We started going round and round, and if you looked out of the bucket, you could see for miles and miles. The buckets weren't enclosed, which was even more fun.

Then from out of nowhere a small wasp landed on my arm. Well, I was no sissy, and I wasn't about to look scared in front of all the girls, so I watched it as it began to crawl up my arm and onto my neck. It crawled onto my cheek, and by now all the girls were watching. It crawled closer and closer to my eye. Finally, I couldn't stand it anymore, and I tried to brush it away. Yep, it stung me with a vengeance. My sister Jenny started yelling that I had been stung and I was allergic. (I'm not allergic to wasps, just weeds. But to her it was all the same.) The wheel came to an abrupt stop and one of the workers grabbed me and started running across the park to the first aid station, with all my sisters close behind. As I looked up, I could see my mom at the top of the Ferris wheel, hanging out of the bucket yelling, "That's my son, get me down!" Part of me found that hilarious.

Growing up in the mountains gave me great appreciation and respect for wildlife. I saw myriad animals—deer, elk, moose, coyotes, mountain lions, bobcats, wild turkeys, red-tailed hawks, and golden eagles, to name a few. I liked watching the wildlife, but I was never much of a hunter. My dad didn't hunt, and I never saw any reason to shoot something that was so beautiful. (Heavy D went deer hunting one time and missed a big high school party that weekend. He never went hunting again.)

I did enjoy fishing, however, and every summer I made a trip to Alaska with Brian and Bruce Kelly, who lived in our neighborhood. We drove six days to Wasilla, Alaska, which is located on the Cook Inlet in the southern part of the state. It's where Sarah Palin lives; she was the town's mayor before she became Alaska's governor and a U.S. vice presidential candidate. Standing in a river in Alaska, in the great American outdoors, watching eagles fly through the sky is something I'll never forget. It was so peaceful; we'd catch enough halibut and king salmon—I caught a 75-pound king salmon on one trip—to fill the freezer for the winter. Because my dad was a Delta pilot, I'd fly standby on a plane headed home and bring the frozen fish with me so they wouldn't spoil.

I acquired my first dirt bike when I was twelve. Our neighbors up the street gave a pair of 1971 Kawasaki KX 100 dirt bikes to my buddies and me. (Did you notice that I had much better taste in rides than Heavy D even at a young age? Unlike him, I never owned a Yamaha bike when I was a kid.) The bikes were old and hadn't been ridden in years, so we had to clean out the carburetors because the gasoline was gelled. It didn't take us very long to get them running, though. I thought we'd done a complete engine overhaul, but they really only needed a little TLC. Of course, there were only two dirt bikes and three of us, so one of us was always riding on the back of a bike.

Where we lived, the asphalt turned into a dirt road that went straight up the mountain. It was like heaven. Nearly every day after school and almost every morning in the summer, I'd ride my dirt bike up the mountain and not come back until it was close to dark, usually with our dog, Cinnamon, a cocker spaniel mix, following me. Unfortunately, she loved chasing cars, and when one of the cars finally won, we adopted a black Labrador retriever named Blackbeary (or Bear for short).

My parents were strict disciplinarians. I guess with seven

kids, they had to put the hammer down to keep us in line. The most important rule they enforced was that we were always expected home before the streetlights came on. It might seem like a simple rule to follow, but sometimes I broke it if my dirt bike ran out of gas or one of the tires went flat (or maybe I was just having too much fun). When I was in high school, my curfew was a little bit later. I had to be home before the chimes on my mom's grandfather clock sounded. If I had to be home at eleven o'clock, and I walked into the door after my parents heard the chimes, I was in trouble. They usually didn't say anything to me that night, but when I woke up the next morning, there was a long list of chores waiting for me. It included things like cleaning the gutters, building rock walls, and doing landscaping. At the time, I didn't know learning how to do those things would help me earn a living when I was older.

If my parents ran out of things for me to do before they thought I'd been punished long enough, which was usually a couple of weeks, they had me move railroad crossties from one side of the yard to the other—just because they told me to do it—or I'd pull weeds on the side of the mountain (on land they didn't even own). No questions asked, I moved them and pulled them. Sometime later I heard my mom and dad discussing why my mom was always inventing chores. She said, "Honey, we don't live on a farm where there is always work to be done. I want to teach our children how to work and work hard.

I want to teach our children how to work and work hard.

So I make up things to do so they know every day you should work some, play some, and feel a sense of accomplishment." Well, the whole lot of us know how to work, that's for sure. Thanks, Mom!

I attended Davis High School in Kaysville, the big rival of Layton High, which is where Heavy D went to school. Even though we didn't live that far apart, we didn't become good friends until after high school (more on that later). I played on the football team and rugby team with Keaton Hoskins, aka "The Muscle," who is part of our crew at Diesel Brothers. I've known The Muscle since the sixth grade. The rugby team was only a club sport, but it was my favorite sport to play. Rugby is a lot like American football, but it's played by real men—and without shoulder pads, helmets, and other padding. In rugby, the field is bigger, the halves are longer, the cuts are deeper, and the bruises are nastier. It's a real man's sport, there's no doubt about it, and I absolutely loved playing it.

My body also took quite a beating from wakeboarding, motocross, and snowboarding. I had four really good friends in my neighborhood—Jason, Matt, and Tyler Erickson and their cousin Jeff Prince—and we were all extremists when it came to sports. We liked to watch videos of Travis Pastrana riding a dirt bike, or Shaun Murray riding a wakeboard, or Jeremy Jones riding a snowboard. Then we'd go out and try to duplicate what they were doing. Of course, those dudes were world champions in their respective sports and had years of training. We were amateurs, to say the least, but that didn't scare us from trying gnarly tricks and mimicking them while wakeboarding at Willard Lake or Pineview Reservoir, and snowboarding at Snowbasin Resort or Powder Mountain.

Needless to say, I suffered quite a few nasty spills. I broke my collarbone a couple of times on a dirt bike, which kept me from joining the army years later, but I considered myself lucky. I had buddies who broke their arms and femurs. It's probably a good thing that I went on a mission for the Church of Jesus Christ of Latter-day Saints right after high school, or I might not have made it out of my teenage years alive!

It's probably a good thing that I went on a mission for the Church of Jesus Christ of Latter-day Saints right after high school, or I might not have made it out of my teenage years alive!

I was probably as much of a gearhead as Heavy D when I was growing up. I liked shop class and working on cars, but I had other interests, mainly girls. My first car was a white 1985 Chrysler Fifth Avenue, which was a gift to me from a family friend. Since I'd learned the basics of auto mechanics in shop class, my buddies and I immediately decided to take the doors off the car. There was something rebellious about riding around in a car with no doors. And it was risky riding around in a car that sat so low to the ground; one T-bone with another car would have taken the whole lot of us out. Once we took the doors off, my parents informed me that I could only

Once we took the doors off, my parents informed me that I could only drive the car if I didn't have to go through an intersection. Oh, the fun suckers.

drive the car if I didn't have to go through an intersection. Oh, the fun suckers.

We put the doors back on, but they never opened or shut the same way again. It was a great car, and I was happy to have a set of wheels. It took quite a bit of time and effort to keep it running, to say the least.

In high school, I practically lived in the Ericksons' house. We were always working on trucks and dirt bikes, and there were boxes of motorcycle and truck parts stacked up in their basement. One time, Jason bought an old Toyota Land Cruiser that looked like a mail truck or ice cream truck. We turned it into a four-wheeling machine and built it in his garage. The Erickson brothers and I had the attitude that we were going to try to figure things out on our own, but their dad, John, knew how to do everything. He was usually shaking his head as he watched us take everything apart.

When I graduated from high school in 2002, I didn't really know what I wanted to do with my life. I knew I wanted to travel and see the world. I liked to build things. I knew I didn't want to have a desk job, where I'd be sitting in an office from nine to five, five days a week, that's for sure.

I wanted to be outside, getting dirty, and using my hands.

That didn't appeal to me at all. I wanted to be outside, getting dirty, and using my hands.

That fall and winter after high school, I worked as a snowboard instructor at Powder Mountain. When the snow melted the next spring, I didn't do much of anything until it was warm enough to go wakeboarding again.

Like Heavy D, I'd committed to a two-year mission with the Church of Jesus Christ of Latter-day Saints. My dad joined the LDS church when he was eighteen, and going on a mission was something he taught us kids about when we were growing up. At the time, I was nineteen years old and was a kid who only thought about himself, and who was only worried about going wakeboarding, snowboarding, or riding a dirt bike every day. I was only living for the thrill of my own life.

I was only living for the thrill of my own life.

To give up all of that and go help someone else seemed like it would be a really cool experience for me. It was an opportunity to learn a lot about how the world works, how to work hard, and how to love somebody else other than myself. I knew it was time for me to grow up. In the fall of 2003, I walked away from everything I'd ever known and prepared for a new life in Lisbon, Portugal. I have to admit I really didn't know what to expect.

DIESEL HANDBOOK LESSON NO. 2
CUMMINS, DURAMAX, OR POWER STROKE?

Hey, we're all a little biased when it comes to certain things. I might like hamburgers from McDonald's, while Diesel Dave prefers Burger King and Redbeard (that's Josh Stuart, one of our coworkers and best friends) likes Wendy's. We also each have our personal favorites when it comes to our sports teams, tennis shoes, candy bars, or whatever.

Diesel engines are no different. Choosing the best diesel engine is one of the most debated and discussed topics in the diesel truck world. Chevrolet and GMC fans prefer the Duramax, Ford drivers like the Power Stroke, and Dodge Ram owners swear by the Cummins. And chances are you're not going to change anyone's mind about the best diesel engine because everyone is firmly set in their beliefs. It's like asking a Dallas Cowboys fan to cheer for the Washington Redskins. It's not going to happen!

We've used each of the diesel engines in various applications, but I've made it pretty clear that I'm a Cummins guy. I have a soft place in my heart for the old Detroit two-strokes, but as far as an engine for an everyday driver and tow rig you can't beat the torque curve of a Cummins. With the right setup, you're at 1,800 rpm pulling 40,000 pounds and you just keep going. Your engine hasn't even broken a sweat yet! Cummins engines want to run and run and run. With nearly 900 foot pounds of torque, they have plenty of power to do any job.

And it certainly helps that Cummins diesel engines have been around the longest. Clessie Lyle Cummins founded the company in Columbus, Indiana, in 1919, and ten years later he produced America's first diesel-powered automobile when he mounted a diesel engine in a used Packard limousine. Cummins started supplying its B-series diesel engines for Dodge Ram pickups in 1989. In 1996, Cummins exceeded 200 horsepower for the first time, and in 2001 it surpassed 500 foot pounds torque. In 2007, Dodge introduced a 6.7-liter engine that produced 350 horsepower, and it reached 385 horsepower and 850 foot pounds torque in 2013.

According to Cummins, more than 75 percent of all Dodge Ram 2500 and 3500 heavy-duty pickup truck owners choose the optional Cummins Turbo Diesel. And Cummins also claims there are more than 100 of its engines that have exceeded 1,000,000 miles still running. How's that for durability? The current Cummins 6.7-liter Turbo Diesel I-6 diesel engine is rated at 370 horsepower at 2,800 rpm and 800 foot pounds torque at 1,700 rpm. Now that's strong!

But like I said earlier, I like all of the diesel engines, and we've used them all in our various builds. Ford primarily uses the Power Stroke diesel engines in its trucks, SUVs, vans, and commercial vehicles. Navistar International Corporation (formerly International Harvester Company) started supplying diesel engines for Ford ¾- and 1-ton trucks in 1982. In 1994, the Ford Power Stroke diesel engines were introduced to emphasize the switch to direct injection. The last Navistar/International Harvester diesel engines were included in Ford trucks in 2010. Ford diesel 6.0-liter engines from 2003 to 2007 had myriad problems with the fuel system, turbochargers, and other major components, so Ford ended its partnership and designed its own diesel engines.

When Ford redesigned its Super Duty trucks in 2011, it introduced its 6.7-liter, V-8 diesel engines that are manufactured in Mexico. According to Ford, more than 500,000 of those engines were sold in its first three years of production. The most recent version of the Ford Turbo Diesel 6.7-liter, V-8 engines is rated at a whopping 860 foot pounds torque at 1,600 rpm and 440 horsepower at 2,800 rpm. After some serious problems, Ford has rebounded and produced a really quality engine with good fuel mileage, power, and towing capacity.

In 1978, General Motors was the first company to introduce diesel engines in its pickup trucks. The Detroit Diesel V-8 engines were pretty solid. In 1998, GM and Isuzu combined forces to develop the first high-pressure, common-rail, direct-injection diesel engines in the United States. The 6.6-liter Duramax V-8 debuted in 2001 with 300 horsepower and 520 foot pounds of torque. The current version of the Duramax 6.6-liter

LML Turbo Diesel engine has 397 horsepower at 3,000 rpm and 765 foot pounds of torque at 1,600 rpm.

Look, if I am buying a diesel truck for the first time, I'm probably going with something that has a Cummins in it. It's the most durable and versatile diesel engine in the world. But Ford, Chevrolet, and General Motors are surely catching up to Dodge as well. Like I told you earlier, it probably goes back to your personal preference.

—Heavy D

CHAPTER THREE
MISSION TRIPS

DIESEL DAVE: In this chapter, Heavy D and I wanted to share a few stories from our mission trips with the Church of Jesus Christ of Latter-day Saints. Obviously, our trips were memorable experiences and important parts of our lives. I promise you'll be reading about building diesel trucks and our unforgettable pranks before too long. But I think to fully understand who we are and how we became such good friends, you need to hear about those experiences, because they really shaped who we are today.

Regardless of where you live, no matter the city, country, or continent, you might have encountered a couple of well-dressed guys walking or bicycling down the street. They might have been wearing backpacks or maybe they were carrying books in their hands. Chances are that Mormon missionaries have probably knocked on your door once or twice over the years. We believe Jesus Christ admonished his disciples to take the gospel to the world, so we send missionaries throughout the world. Maybe you slammed the door in their faces after they introduced themselves, or maybe you were kind, welcomed them inside your home, and listened to what they had to say.

Coming from a pair of guys who knocked on literally thousands of doors during their two-year mission trips to southern Europe and South America, we sincerely thank you if you're part of the latter group. Obviously, we realize it might be hard to imagine that we were once LDS missionaries when you look at us now. But it wasn't too long ago that we were clean-shaved, well-dressed, and on a mission to save the world through God's word.

But it wasn't too long ago that we were clean-shaven, well dressed, and on a mission to save the world through God's word.

And believe us—we had quite a few doors slammed in our faces.

I'll never forget one lady in Lisbon, Portugal, who didn't seem too interested in what my companion and I were trying to share with her. After my senior companion introduced us, she immediately frowned and tried to slam her door. But the door wouldn't close and swung back toward her.

"Get your foot out of my door," she told my companion, before she tried to slam the door even harder. Once again, the door kicked back and nearly hit her in the face.

"Get your foot out of my door!" she repeated, as she pushed the door with even more strength.

"Ma'am," I finally told her in my best but not-yet-polished Portuguese, "your door will shut completely if you'd kindly remove your cat."

Jokes aside, faith is very important to Heavy D and me. In fact, it's the most important aspect of our lives and the entire reason for our being. Faith is what brought us together and it's what made our company what it is today.

> Faith is what brought us together and it's what made our company what it is today.

As we told you earlier, we both grew up in the LDS church, and we still attend services every Sunday morning. We met our wives through church, and we even became best friends after attending an LDS function for singles.

Basically, Mormons believe that the Church of Jesus Christ of Latter-day Saints is the restored church of Jesus Christ on earth. We believe in modern-day prophets, that someone receives guidance from God to guide His church. We believe the church is exactly the same as it was when Jesus Christ was on this earth, so we have sacrament and believe in the sacrifice of Jesus for the sins of the world. We are very committed to our faith. We abstain from alcohol, tobacco, and other drugs. We don't believe in premarital sex and try not to curse.

We believe that through Jesus Christ we can live with him again someday. But the main focus of the LDS church is the family unit, and we believe that you, the person you marry, your kids, your parents, and everybody close to you can be sealed together. That means the family unit will be a family unit in the next life as well. Family is the foundation for this life and the life to come. That's the message we carry to the world, and it's a message of hope and inspiration.

Serving a mission trip is not a requirement of the LDS church, but it's pushed pretty hard because of the experiences you'll have. As a member of the church, you grow up thinking about how you're going to have this experience when you're old enough. It's a tremendous sacrifice. I'm not sure people fully understand the commitment that comes with a two-year LDS mission.

During your mission trip, you're only allowed to call home two times a year—on Mother's Day and Christmas. You can write letters home every week, but you can only hear your loved ones' voices twice per year. You don't have a phone or computer and have no real connection to the outside world. You can't listen to music. You can't get in the water unless you're baptizing someone, so we couldn't go swimming even in a place where it was nearly 90 degrees every day of the year. You can't touch girls—you can't even talk to girls. You become a full-on monk.

You can't touch girls—you can't even talk to girls. You become a full-on monk.

I left for my mission trip in February 2003. While I was waiting for my visa to travel to Portugal, I spent three months at the Minnesota Minneapolis Mission in Bloomington, Minnesota. Unfortunately, I was there in the middle of the winter. I've never been so cold in my life. On some days, if you walked outside, your nose hairs literally froze. I'm not kidding—it was that cold. Obviously, Lisbon is a little warmer than Minnesota, so I had to trade my winter clothes for cooler ones when I finally left for the Iberian Peninsula.

When you get thrown into a country where people don't speak the same language as you, it's a culture shock. You spend the first few months learning the language and relying heavily on a translator. But by the fourth month, you start understanding what people are saying. You even start dreaming in a new language. It's an unreal experience. That's probably been one of the biggest blessings of our lives, learning to speak another language.

I was lucky in more ways than one when it came to my mission. It's a rare occurrence to know others serving at the same place, but there were two guys from my neighborhood— Ferin Prince and John Thompson—who were in Lisbon with me. They were about a year younger than me, but I knew them and it was good to see familiar faces. I was also very fortunate to be assigned to Lisbon, which is a coastal city and one of the oldest (Christopher Columbus was marooned there in the late fifteenth century) and most beautiful cities in Europe. The city is filled with iconic castles, towers, arches, and cathedrals. It was one of the most beautiful places I've ever been, and it really stoked my desire to see other parts of the world.

It was fun and fulfilling to go out in the world and preach a happy message to people who were really in a hard place. We met a lot of people who were struggling. Maybe they lost someone they loved and were grieving, and we tried to deliver them hope through our message. We met people living in the streets and shelters, and we might have helped build them a house or repaired the one where they were living to try to get them on their feet. During my mission trip to Portugal, I replaced roofs, rebuilt walls, cleaned parks and streets, and knocked on plenty of doors. Basically, wherever you thought you could lend a hand, you put yourself there and went to work. I had the opportunity not only to share with people my belief in the restored Church of Jesus Christ, and a modern-day prophet on earth, but also to serve and help people. We strongly believe in the two great commandments: Love Thy God and Love Thy Neighbor. I know for a fact the world would be a much better place if people would only love and serve their neighbors.

I know for a fact the world would be a much better place if people would only love and serve their neighbors.

During my mission, we focused on serving people and helping them with whatever needs they had to lighten their burdens. We have a firm belief that if you work your tail off and put your faith in God, He will answer your prayers, lighten your burdens, and help you accomplish the things you need to be happy.

One person I remember helping in particular was Mugurel, who was a young man from Romania. He had no place to live after he lost his job and so was living on the streets. He was a twenty-year-old guy, my age at the time, and his entire life was in front of him. We didn't go on mission trips with much money, but the other missionaries and I threw together what we had and paid for a hotel room for him. We tried to help find him work, and even bought him a shoe-shining kit to keep him busy while he searched for a better job. Mugurel was trying hard, but he was understandably becoming desperate. No one would hire an undocumented immigrant from Romania.

Once Mugurel's money ran out, he was evicted from his hotel room, so we put a mattress on the floor in our hallway and let him sleep there. We prayed each night that he would find work and a place to live. We didn't want our friend living on the streets. Well, as proof that God answers prayers, we received a telephone call the next day and learned that Mugurel had found a job and a place to live! He was hired as a carpenter only a couple of towns over. We helped him pack his things and found him a ride to his new apartment. He had a big smile on his face and newly found zeal in his life.

I learned that it's the little things in life that make a huge impact, like being a friend and helping people when they really need it. I had lots of experiences in my mission in which I had the opportunity to make new friends and serve them. I grew to love the people of Portugal, and I learned to love people in general. In a world with so much negativity, it makes a tremendous difference to help lift people up, instead of tearing them down. Try bringing positivity and happiness into the world, instead of the opposite. You'll be surprised how much it changes your own life.

HEAVY D: In February 2004, I spent three weeks at the Missionary Training Center in Provo, Utah, and then six weeks at another training center in Lima, Peru. I was paired with a Latin companion, who started to teach me Spanish since our mission was going to be to Santa Cruz, Bolivia.

When we reached Bolivia, we were dropped right in the middle of the Amazon rain forest. We served the people of Riberalta, a town of about 78,000 residents. From what I remember, there were about five brick houses in the entire town, and the rest of the residents lived in dwellings made of bamboo, mud, and grass. The good news is we could build one of those bamboo houses in about three days, which was often our service project.

It seemed like everyone in Riberalta, except for maybe the young children and senior citizens, worked in the rain forest harvesting Brazil nuts, which are found in fruits that resemble five-pound cannonballs. And let me tell you: the fruits sound like cannonballs being shot from a cannon when they fall from the trees! The nuts are harvested when the fruits are cut open with machetes. Nearly every day, I followed the workers into the jungle, wearing a white shirt, tie, and backpack, carrying the *Book of Mormon*, and searching for someone to teach.

On my one day off each week, I'd do my laundry and spend thirty minutes writing a letter to my parents.

> *Nearly every day, I followed the workers into the jungle, wearing a white shirt, tie, and backpack, carrying the Book of Mormon, and searching for someone to teach.*

After I had spent about a year in Bolivia, my mission president decided he was going to send me to a town in West Brazil, where there hadn't been a missionary in twenty years. I had to learn another language because they spoke Portuguese there. In two years in Bolivia and Brazil, I helped baptize about 150 people.

For two years, you're never alone—no matter what, you have to be in sight of your companion, who is another LDS missionary and accompanies you throughout your mission. That's the number one rule for missionaries. You get a new companion about every six weeks. I had nineteen different companions in two years, and most of them were from Latin America or South America. Many of them came from impoverished backgrounds. We'd get a weekly allowance for food, and while I was trying to figure out how I was going to survive on so little, many of them had never had so much food to eat. Our weekly allowance might have been more than their families earned in a month. You definitely learned a lot about being humble and being grateful for what we have.

> *You definitely learned a lot about being humble and being grateful for what we have.*

The families of LDS missionaries also make a tremendous sacrifice. For two years they are separated from their loved ones and have very little contact with them. Because of the way our ages are staggered, my brother, my sisters, and I were each on mission trips around the same time. During a six-year period, at least three of my parents' four children were concurrently on mission trips outside the United States, which wasn't easy for them.

My oldest sister, Michelle, did her mission in Rio de Janeiro, Brazil, and my other sister, Alicia, was assigned to the Canary Islands. My brother, Taylor, went to Argentina. It was cool when we came back because my siblings and I could talk to each other in Spanish, and my parents couldn't understand what we were saying.

My faith is important to me. It means that there is more to this life than what meets the eye. In the grand scheme of things, this life is just a drop in the bucket and what we do here determines where we go and what we do in the life that's after this. My faith gives me a reason to live and a reason to live by certain guidelines and set of rules. It makes me want to be a good person and helps me understand what the benefits are and what the eternal consequences are for being a good person.

One of the biggest things it's helped me learn and understand is that even though I might be important and have a high self-worth, everyone, including me, is equally important. Others' needs are just as important as mine. It has taught me the concepts of charity and service, and thinking less about myself and more about other people's needs. It's what my dad would have wanted from me.

CHAPTER FOUR
HUMBLE BEGINNING

DIESEL DAVE: Hey, let's face it: some people were born to be together: Tom & Jerry, Batman & Robin, Han Solo & Chewbacca, Bert & Ernie, Mario & Luigi, and Ben & Jerry (one of my personal favorites), to name a few. Sure, some of those folks would be great by themselves, but they're way better and so much more fun when they're together. I mean, seriously, what would Brad Pitt be without Angelina Jolie? Wait, never mind.

Look at the greatest sports duos of all time. Just like Scooby-Doo needed Shaggy, Magic Johnson needed Kareem Abdul-Jabbar, and Karl Malone needed John Stockton. Michael Jordan would have still been the GOAT without Scottie Pippen, and Joe Montana would have probably been a Hall of Famer without Jerry Rice, but those guys were so much better as pairs.

I know one thing: none of those people started a lifelong

friendship and partnership like Heavy D and me. We became best friends when I was forced to correct one of the biggest blunders of his life—and it was not an enjoyable experience!

> *We became best friends when I was forced to correct one of the biggest blunders of his life—and it was not an enjoyable experience!*

First, let me give you a little bit of background about how we actually met for the first time. Remember what I said about me being restless? Well, when I finished my two-year LDS mission to Portugal in 2005, I was offered a job working as a sheet metal fabricator for a heating, ventilation, and air-conditioning company in California—on the very day I went back to Utah. I accepted the job and left home a few days later, much to my lovely mother's dismay.

Don't get me wrong—I love my mom dearly. I read somewhere that the definition of a mother is "someone who will love you unconditionally till her last breath." Think about it: Your first relationship in the world is with your mom, and she's always going to be there and love you no matter what. Regardless of what we might do and how we treat our mothers, they're still going to love us. That's unconditional love, all right.

I can promise you one thing: my mother, Kellee Kiley, loves me unconditionally, no matter what I have done. Even though my mom was upset about me leaving home again so soon, she understood my decision because I needed a job and needed to start my life as an adult. But let's just say I didn't win any "Son of the Year" awards in the Kiley household for quite a while.

I moved to Los Angeles and lived about two miles from the Santa Monica Pier. It was a great place to live and there was so much to do. Unfortunately, I didn't have time to surf or do anything else because I was working so much. We were installing an HVAC system at the Mormon temple in Los Angeles, working eighteen hours a day. It was grueling and exhausting work, but I was making good money. At that point in my life, my entire purpose was to work hard until I'd saved enough money to travel to some faraway land (more on that later).

When I was living in Los Angeles, I tried to get back home on the weekends as often as possible—my dad was working as a pilot for Delta, so I could fly standby for free—so my mother eventually forgave me. During one trip home, I rode dirt bikes in the mountains with my buddies, just like we used to do as kids. Unfortunately, I wrecked my bike and broke my collarbone. I couldn't lift anything for several weeks, so I had to quit my job in L.A. and move back to Utah.

I lived with my parents for a while and then moved into a house in Salt Lake City with six other guys in 2006. That's when I met Heavy D for the first time. He was hanging out with the Erickson brothers, my good friends, and they liked to call him "Replacement Dave." When I was living in California, all I heard about was this other dude named Dave. They said we were so much alike it was almost as if we were brothers from another mother.

They said we were so much alike it was almost as if we were brothers from another mother.

After I moved back to Utah, I went to a party for Mormon singles one night, and I saw the other Dave walking down the stairs. It was almost as if there was going to be a showdown—like the one between Arnold Schwarzenegger and the Predator—right there in the middle of the living room. Hey, Salt Lake City wasn't big enough for both of us. Instead, something clicked between Heavy D and me, and we became very good friends almost immediately. We both enjoyed going to the lake and riding dirt bikes, and he was already hanging out with all of my friends anyhow.

A couple of days after that party, Heavy D invited me to go wakeboarding and skiing at the lake with him. He was taking a few of his other friends, including a handful of girls. That was more than enough reason for me to go. He picked me up in his 2002 Chevy 2500 diesel truck, which he had recently purchased to pull his boat. We loaded up in his truck and headed for the lake. When we stopped at a convenience store for fuel, I glanced out the window and noticed Heavy D was pumping gasoline into his diesel truck. Now, I'd never owned a diesel vehicle, but even I knew you weren't supposed to put regular gasoline in a diesel. It's like eating French fries with mayonnaise.

Now, I'd never owned a diesel vehicle, but even I knew you weren't supposed to put regular gasoline in a diesel. It's like eating French fries with mayonnaise.

They don't mix, brother!

I jumped out of the truck and tried to play it cool, so the

girls wouldn't sense that something was wrong. "Hey, man, aren't you supposed to be using the green handle?" I asked him.

Immediately, Heavy D slapped his forehead and realized his mistake. He hadn't filled up his diesel tank completely, but he'd pumped enough gasoline into the truck where he didn't want to run his engine. We called another buddy, who came and picked up the girls. Obviously, we weren't going to the lake that day.

Then came the unforgettable moment when Heavy D and I became best friends for life. Over the course of the next couple of hours, I helped him siphon about fifteen to twenty gallons of gasoline out of his truck—using our mouths and a garden hose. It really sucked, if you know what I mean.

Because of that act of courage and selflessness, Heavy D hired me to work with him at his landscaping company. I guess he figured any guy who was willing to suck gasoline out of a diesel truck was worth keeping around. It was the start of a great friendship and even bigger adventures together.

HEAVY D: Oh, please don't think Diesel Dave forgot about my tiny mistake so easily. He only brought it up every day for the next three or four months. In fact, he seemingly lived to share the details of the time I put gasoline in my diesel truck with anyone who was willing to listen. I think it's still his favorite story to share, but it wasn't very long before karma bit him in the rear end.

About six months before my LDS mission trip in Brazil

ended, my uncle John Tanner wrote me a letter, asking me to work for his construction company as a foreman when I returned home. The real estate market was booming in Salt Lake City at the time, and houses were going up everywhere. As I mentioned earlier, I worked with my uncle and grandfather in high school, and working for them full-time would afford me an opportunity to learn and master a lot of new skills.

I still thought I might end up working as a mechanic one day, but construction was a good job and the money allowed me to buy my first full-sized truck (yes, the diesel one). I also enrolled in night classes at Weber State University, which is where my dad went to school. I took two classes my first semester—communications and environmental appreciation.

One night, while I was sitting in class writing a term paper about Easter Island, I stopped and asked myself what I was doing there. Then I turned to the guy sitting next to me and asked, "Are we ever going to use this in real life?" The kid stared at me and didn't say a word. He didn't have an answer, either, and it really bothered me. So I left class that night and never went back. I determined that having an academic degree wasn't that important to me. That's one thing about me: when I don't like something, I just stop doing it—on a dime. Ask my wife about me helping with laundry and cleaning the gutters, if you don't believe me.

That's one thing about me: when I don't like something, I just stop doing it—on a dime. Ask my wife about me helping with laundry and cleaning the gutters, if you don't believe me.

For the next two years, I continued building houses with my uncle and grandfather. Then the Great Recession hit in 2008 and home construction came to a screeching halt. My uncle had to lay off most of his crews and even his nephew wasn't immune. There wasn't any work for anybody. Even with the houses we'd already started, the developers came to us and said, "We don't have any money; stop building them." So the houses sat there, half-finished and empty, for several years.

Now, the silver lining in this story is that my uncle owned a lot of heavy equipment that was sitting idle. He told me I could use his tractors to find odd jobs, as long as I paid for the fuel and kept them maintained. He had two Case tractors—an excavator and smaller skid loader—that I ended up borrowing. I advertised my services in the newspaper and charged about $300 to $400 per job. I wasn't licensed and wasn't insured, but I had two tractors and a truck to pull them.

At first, we built rock walls and crosstie walls and completed other smaller landscaping and maintenance jobs. We had a different name for our company depending on the day and the job; it really depended on what we were doing. On the days we built rock walls it was D&D Landscaping. On the days we built fences it was D&D Fences. On the days we built waterfalls it was D&D Waterfalls. It didn't matter the name or the job, we were going to find a way to do it.

With every new job, it seemed like we bit off a little more than we could chew. When one of my mom's friends wanted a really high-end waterfall built at her house, I presented her with what I thought was a ridiculously high bid. Much to my surprise, she accepted our bid (she later told me it was one-quarter of what every other contractor wanted), and we built her a waterfall, even though we really had no idea what we were doing. Somehow, it actually turned out pretty nice and she loved it. Word was spreading about our company, and then we really started getting busy.

That's about the time I hired Diesel Dave to work with us. I operated the excavator, and he drove the skid loader. Our third employee was "Jackknife" Jim Anderson, who still works with us at DieselSellerz today. Diesel Dave became our employee of the month when he completed a front flip with the skid loader—it was a miracle he wasn't hurt. And then I finally quit hearing about the time I pumped gasoline into my diesel truck when he poured diesel into the hydraulic fluid tank on the skid loader. After hearing about my mistake for so long, I wasn't much help getting diesel out of the loader.

By 2010, we were really starting to land some big jobs. We built a 100-foot waterfall at one house, which took us several weeks to complete. In the end, the contractor never paid us for our work, which really set us back financially. I spent about $5,000 renting the equipment to complete the job, and then I was stuck with the bill. On our next job, we were hired to dig out a full basement and remove the old foundation. When we were about 90 percent done with the job and tearing down the last wall, I damaged the boom of the excavator, which was worth about $75,000. There was a $10,000 repair bill, and I didn't have insurance. At the time, it seemed like all the money in the world to me.

Needless to say, it wiped our company (and me) out financially. We didn't have enough capital to stay afloat, and we ended up calling it a day. Diesel Dave and I were both in our mid-twenties, and we really didn't have any idea where our lives were headed.

DIESEL HANDBOOK LESSON NO. 3
TRUCK HUNTING

So you've saved your money and you're ready to buy your first diesel truck. Congratulations! You're about to join a rare breed of Americans who like to work hard all week and play harder on the weekends.

You're also about to make one of the biggest purchases of your life, so it's important to know what you should be looking for when you go to look at a used diesel truck.

Here are a few key factors to keep in mind:

1. Check the Carfax report.

If you're considering buying a used diesel truck, it's a good idea to ask for the vehicle identification number (VIN) to check the Carfax report, which will tell you if the truck has been wrecked or salvaged. It can also give you a fairly accurate odometer reading that you can compare to what's showing up on the truck.

In some cases, the Carfax report will tell you how regularly the truck was serviced at dealerships. Plus, ownership details in the report might reveal whether the truck was ever registered in the Northeast or Midwest, where it might have been exposed to salt used for deicing roads, which might lead to rust on the vehicle. I try to avoid buying trucks from those areas.

2. Do a walk-around.

If the Carfax report is satisfactory, set up an appointment to see the truck and do a thorough inspection. Ask to see the truck's maintenance records; you're probably going to have better luck getting them from an individual seller than a dealership.

Walk around the truck and look for body damage and other wear and tear. Are there cracks in the windows? Check to see if the seams where the hood closes are properly aligned, and if there's equal spacing where the doors and fenders meet.

Open and close the doors to see if they're bent. Make sure the bumpers are on straight, and look behind the weather stripping in the doors to see if the truck has been painted again. That's another sign that the truck might have been wrecked.

Here's another tip: Bring a magnet with you and randomly try to adhere it to the sheet metal on the truck. If it doesn't stick, there was probably shoddy bodywork done in the past.

3. Raise the hood.

If you like what you see during the walk-around, raise the hood and inspect the engine. Check the oil and transmission fluid levels. If the oil appears to be gooey or black or if you see shiny metallic particles in it, you don't want to buy the truck. Smell the transmission fluid to see if it smells burnt. If it does, the truck probably has a transmission problem.

Before you start the engine, squeeze the hoses to see if they feel stiff or brittle. Are the hoses properly clamped? Are there cracks in any of the belts? Are the battery cables corroded? Check the purchase date on the battery to see if it's really old. Also, examine the coolant reserve to see if it's clean. You can find out a lot about how a truck has been serviced and maintained by the condition of the fluids.

4. Turn everything on.

Before you go for a test drive, turn the key but don't start the engine. Make sure all of the warning lights show up, including the check-engine and supplemental restraint system lights. Believe it or not, some people turn those lights off to cover up needed repairs.

Check to make sure the air conditioning, defrost, radio, locks, windshield wipers, power mirrors, headlights, and windows are all functioning properly. If there's a sunroof in the truck, make sure it opens and closes correctly.

This is important: Make sure you start the engine cold. You want to be able to see if it starts sluggishly, or if white or black smoke comes out of the exhaust. White smoke indicates there might be an issue with the glow plugs; black smoke means something might be wrong with the injectors.

Once you're driving the truck, pay attention to whether or not there are vibrations or if the engine is skipping. Does the engine knock as you accelerate? Does the engine feel tired and worn? Do the brakes vibrate when you use them? Does the cruise control work? Punch it a few times to make sure the transmission is shifting into gears and overdrive smoothly. It's a good idea to take the truck to a parking lot and make sharp turns to make sure there's no rubbing, clicking, or resistance in the steering wheel.

5. Look for leaks.

Once you're done driving the truck, wait about ten minutes and then look under it to see if there are any leaks. Look for oil, transmission fluid, or antifreeze. If you used the air-conditioning, there's probably going to be some water dripping from condensation, which is normal. Also, look under the hood to see if you hear a hissing noise, which is a sign that the engine is running hot.

Check the pressure in the tires and make sure there's no curb damage on the wheels. Are the tires wearing evenly? Are any lug nuts missing? Also look for signs of corrosion in the wheel wells.

6. Take the truck to a mechanic.

If you're not a mechanic or don't have access to a lift, it's a good idea to take the truck to a repair shop to have it inspected. If a dealership is selling the truck, take it to a third-party mechanic so it's an unbiased inspection.

Once the truck is on a lift, a mechanic can check to see if

there's corrosion on the underbody or if the chassis has been cracked or bent. He can check for leaks on the engine bottom, transmission, radiator, and differentials. He can also check the brake pads and rotors to see if they're worn.

A good mechanic will also hook the truck up to a diagnostic code reader, which can read data from the truck's onboard computer and generate error codes, which might lead to needed repairs.

–Heavy D

CHAPTER FIVE
BUCKET LIST

DIESEL DAVE: If you haven't figured it out by now, I really like adventure and trying new things. In fact, I think everybody should have a bucket list. You probably know that a bucket list is a compilation of goals you want to achieve, dreams you want to fulfill, and things you want to experience before you die. A bucket list might include faraway places you want to visit, famous people you want to meet (like Heavy D!), or maybe exotic foods you want to try. A bucket list isn't supposed to be some sort of race against time; it's more about maximizing your time on earth and living life to the fullest, which is something I've always tried to do.

Of course, my bucket list is probably a lot more adventurous than most. Along with growing a beard, getting married, fathering a child, blowing up a Toyota Prius, and trying broccoli for the first time, I wanted to run a marathon, swim with sea life, go bungee jumping, and take a cross-country motorcycle trip.

Along with growing a beard, getting married, fathering a child, blowing up a Toyota Prius, and trying broccoli for the first time, I wanted to run a marathon, swim with sea life, go bungee jumping, and take a cross-country motorcycle trip.

And since I've never been one to take shortcuts, I decided to run a marathon at the Great Wall of China, swim with sharks in South Africa, bungee-jump from Victoria Falls, and drive a motorcycle from Brazil to Utah. (Yeah, you read that right!)

Fortunately for me, when Heavy D's landscaping business folded, I'd saved enough money to travel for a while. (Don't tell him, but I was kind of happy it was time for vacation.) That was my mindset back then—I'd work hard until I'd saved enough money to get back on the road and travel to some exotic place. I didn't buy a lot of material things and tried to keep my expenses to a minimum. I'd try to save every dollar I made to go to some faraway land to learn about a new culture and see new things.

Near the end of the summer in 2009, I traveled to Brazil with three good friends of mine—Jackknife Jim Anderson, Dan Gardner, and Brian "Nian" Allphin. We flew to South America and took a bus to Florianopólis, Brazil, which is where Jim served his Mormon mission. Florianopólis is in the southern part of Brazil and has some of the most beautiful beaches in the world. Most of the city sits on Santa Catarina Island, which is great for surfing, boating, and fishing, which is about all we did there.

When we arrived in Florianópolis, we each bought a motorcycle for about $2,000; we figured we would sell them at the end of our trip and have enough money to buy airline tickets back to the United States. There are no rules when it comes to driving motorcycles in Brazil. You can ride them anywhere— on sidewalks, in between traffic, and on dirt roads through the rain forest. We rode our motorcycles all over Brazil.

At night, we slept in hammocks in the jungle. We ate fruit from trees and bathed in creeks and lakes. (After first checking the water for piranhas and anacondas!) About once a month, we rented a room in a hostel to shower, rest, and wash our clothes. Some of the locals were horrified when they learned we were sleeping in the rain forest. They couldn't believe a puma hadn't eaten us.

> *Some of the locals were horrified when they learned we were sleeping in the rain forest. They couldn't believe a puma hadn't eaten us.*

Looking back now, it's quite remarkable something didn't attack us. We saw alligators and sloths lying on the side of the road, venomous snakes and monkeys in the trees, and yep, even a puma or two stalking its prey in the rain forest. Somebody was watching over us; that's for sure.

When it was time to go home, about two months into our trip, we decided that none of us really had anything to go back to in Salt Lake City. None of us had girlfriends or jobs, so there really wasn't any pressing reason for us to get back to the States. So instead of flying home, we decided we'd keep the motorcycles and drive them all the way back to Utah on the Pan-American Highway. There was no doubt about it: this was going to be the mother of all road trips and one we'd never forget.

There was no doubt about it: this was going to be the mother of all road trips and one we'd never forget.

The trip back home took us through a dozen countries—Brazil, Bolivia, Peru, Ecuador, and Colombia in South America and then Panama, Costa Rica, Nicaragua, Honduras, El Salvador, Guatemala, and Mexico in Central America. The gas-guzzling, knuckle-busting, foot-cramping, dirt-flying road trip covered more than 5,500 miles—and it wasn't a very fast ride, either. My motorcycle traveled about 55 miles per hour if I had the hammer down—and we were going downhill! You couldn't push a 200cc bike very hard. Along the way, I saw a plethora of things I'll never forget, including the Avenue of the Volcanoes and Swing at the End of the World in Ecuador and the Mayan pyramids in Mexico.

Once we reached Colombia, we met a pirate—a living, breathing swashbuckler—who agreed to carry our motorcycles on his boat across the Darien Gap, which is a 100-mile stretch of marshland, jungle, and mountains that doesn't have a road. He covered our bikes with tarps so we wouldn't have to pay import taxes on them, and then he dropped us off in the jungles of Panama.

Around the time we reached Central America, I received an email from my good friend Matt Erickson, who informed me that he was engaged and getting married the next week. We'd been gone for nearly four months and it was time to go home. We put the hammer down on our motorcycles and drove them all the way back to the United States. We arrived in Salt Lake City the day before Matt's wedding and had some unforgettable stories to tell.

I went back to work for Heavy D, who had started a company by buying and selling cars, but I still wasn't settled and yearned for the road. As soon as I made enough money with Dave in the spring of 2010, I went to South Africa, where I swam with sharks and bungee-jumped from the top of Victoria Falls. I don't know if there's a bigger adrenaline rush than being dropped into the ocean in a steel cage, while 2,000-pound great white sharks swim around you. Sharks might look like man-eaters, but they're actually pretty docile animals. I still wouldn't recommend jumping into the ocean with them if you're bleeding, though.

When we went to Victoria Falls, which is located on the border of Zambia and Zimbabwe in southern Africa, our Jeep broke down in the middle of a hippopotamus field. Hippos might be herbivores, but when 4,000-pound animals are roaring loudly and threatening to charge, you can't find cover fast enough. Being dropped 700 feet over one of the world's largest (and most beautiful) waterfalls was also an experience—and rush—I'll never forget.

After spending a couple of months in Africa, I went to China and ran a marathon on the Great Wall. I figured I'd probably run one marathon in my life, so I chose one of the hardest. The Great Wall Marathon in Tianjin Province is considered one of the most grueling races in the world; it covers six kilometers—and more than 5,100 steps—on the wall. The race took me six hours to finish, and it was quite an achievement for someone who really wasn't much of a runner. After the marathon, we traveled to Thailand for some rest and relaxation. That's when Heavy D sent me an email with a photo of a tow truck, and I figured he had something up his sleeve.

HEAVY D: While Diesel Dave was traveling the world, crossing items off his bucket list like Morgan Freeman and Jack Nicholson, I was busy being a grown-up and trying to launch a career—for both of us!

After I closed the doors on my landscaping business, I took a job with Rockwell Watches, which was founded in 2007 by my mentor and good friend Rich Eggett. Rockwell marketed its watches to athletes in sports like surfing, mixed martial arts, motor sports, and sand volleyball. Rockwell sponsored a lot of motocross races and other events, and I drove the company's hauler to sites and sold watches, sunglasses, and other apparel out of the company's trailer. Before too long, I was helping organize events, working with riders and teams that Rockwell sponsored, and identifying other sponsorships.

Rich taught me a lot about business, staging events, and marketing, and I see a lot of Diesel Dave's personality in him.

Before Rich founded his company, he and one of his buddies sold their cars to go run with the bulls in Pamplona, Spain. On the big day, Rich wanted to get a head start—in front of the bulls—but his friend held them back. He told Rich they hadn't come that far to run away from the bulls; they were there to actually run *with* them. Fortunately, they both survived. Rich transformed Rockwell Watches from a small start-up company into an international brand that is endorsed by professional athletes and celebrities around the world.

As much as I enjoyed working for Rockwell, and I'll forever be grateful for the opportunity Rich gave me, I knew I didn't want to spend the rest of my life working for someone else. I was about to get married to my wife, Ashley (more on that later), and I knew I needed to do something on my own to support my family. As a side business, I decided to open a used car dealership. I was familiar with auto mechanics, and I figured I could flip enough cars and trucks to supplement my salary from Rockwell. I started by buying broken-down cars that people had sitting in their backyards—I even hired Diesel Dave to go door-to-door looking for them. To be honest, we were looking for cars that cost only a couple of hundred bucks. Once we got them running again, we sold them and hoped to make about $500 on each vehicle. Obviously, we had to sell quite a few cars and trucks to make any money.

We ended up keeping a few of the vehicles we purchased, which probably wasn't the greatest business model. In fact, we gave Diesel Dave's sister the first car we ever bought. We also purchased a beat-up Chevrolet S-10 pickup truck, spent too much money fixing it, and then decided to keep it as a shop truck. After we saved enough money, we acquired a tow truck for $7,000. Its engine had caught on fire and wasn't running. We spent about $400 to get it working again and used it to buy and sell more vehicles. Our small dealership was growing and we were starting to earn a little money. A lot of our clients were friends and family. Instead of selling them cars, we snuck them into auctions and let them buy vehicles at wholesale instead of retail prices. They paid us about $500 for our services.

Everything was going pretty smoothly until a state agent knocked on my door. Under Utah law at the time, you were only allowed to buy and sell three vehicles per year—unless you were a licensed auto dealer. Well, I wasn't a licensed dealer and to become one, you had to have an actual physical lot with a sign, an office with a filing cabinet (seriously), and a $100,000 bond. Getting a bond wasn't easy. Basically, you had to be a forty-year-old married man with a mortgage and established credit. Obviously, I was none of the above, so I was getting turned down left and right for a bond. It seemed like my career in auto sales was coming to an end.

Fortunately, I had a friend whose brothers, Jeff and Ryan Gardner, were licensed auto dealers. They owned a car dealership named B&W Autos in Provo, Utah, but they weren't doing much with it. They agreed to let me take over the dealership, as long as I kept the books up-to-date. I moved the dealership to Bountiful, Utah, near Salt Lake City. I leased an office for $200 per month, purchased a filing cabinet, and made a sign. We carried about $5,000 in inventory at a time, which wasn't much, but at least it was a start.

Once Diesel Dave finally returned from his world adventures, we partnered with Chris and Jose Lopez and opened our first auto shop in early 2012. We continued to sell junk cars, but we also flipped some pretty nice trucks. The first one was a Dodge Ram 2500 Mega Cab. Long-bed conversions—when you transform a short-bedded truck into a long-bedded one—were pretty popular at the time. A long-bed conversion gives you the best of both worlds: you get a spacious, comfortable cab that seats five adults, and a longer, more functional bed that can carry wallboard, lumber, or whatever you want. Plus, the long-bedded trucks are more equipped to haul heavy trailers, especially when they're being powered by a Cummins 5.9-liter diesel engine.

Even though we didn't know what we were doing when it came to long-bed conversions, we knew it was cool. We cut the short bed off the Dodge Ram 2500 Mega Cab and used our Home Depot tools to attach a long-bed frame we purchased from a salvage yard. Of course, when we attached the long-bed frame, it was crooked and we had to do it over again. We had to get the truck ready to sell, so we cut everything off again and put it back together correctly. We put new wheels and tires on the truck and gave it a six-inch lift. It was a mean and powerful truck when we were finished.

We started a Facebook page called Diesel Trucks For Sale

and advertised the Dodge truck. It was our first truck that went viral—people went nuts over it! In September 2012, we sold the truck for $35,000. The guy who bought it traded in a 2008 Ford F-250, which we flipped and sold for $5,000 profit.

(Hey, this is Diesel Dave again. What Heavy D failed to tell you is that I drew the unenviable assignment of driving the Dodge truck to Georgia to pick up the Ford F-250. For some reason, the guy had painted the headlights on the Ford, so I could barely see when I was driving at night. When I reached Wyoming, something went wrong and the truck wouldn't go faster than 25 miles per hour. I had to drive the last 400 miles that way, and a two-day trip turned into a four-day trip! People who were driving on I-84 must have hated me. When we got the truck back to our shop, we figured out the traction control was whacked. All you had to do was push a button and it would have come out of it. Duh!)

Regardless, it was a real kick-starter for our company. Between the cash the guy in Georgia paid us and the profit we made off his trade-in, it was more money than we'd made off the junk cars combined. Suddenly, Diesel Dave and I realized what we were going to do with the rest of our lives!

CHAPTER SIX
DIESEL POWER

HEAVY D: During the famous cola wars, Pepsi asked American consumers to try the Pepsi Challenge to prove its soft drink tasted better than Coca-Cola. When Wendy's wanted to challenge fast-food giants Burger King and McDonald's, it asked America, "Where's the beef?" And when Nike wanted to soar past upstart Reebok in their fierce tennis shoe war, it signed NBA rookie Michael Jordan to pitch its products. The rest, as they say, is history.

Well, do you know how rednecks decide whether a Ford or Dodge is a more powerful truck? They tie a steel chain to their bumpers and have a tug-of-war in the snow.

Well, do you know how rednecks decide whether a Ford or Dodge is a more powerful truck? They tie a steel chain to their bumpers and have a tug-of-war in the snow.

That's exactly what DieselSellerz did in the very first video we posted to YouTube in March 2013. We chained a 2011 Ford F-350 to a 2010 Dodge 3500 and let the trucks duke it out in a snow-covered parking lot. Like the tug-of-war we played with a rope as kids, the game is over when one truck physically moves the other one (or, in the case of a truck that uses gasoline, when the engine blows, which usually doesn't take very long).

Our stunt wasn't a normal tug-of-war, though. For added special effects, we had the drivers turn the steering wheels, instead of dropping the hammer and pulling straight ahead. As a result, the trucks produced a three-minute donut in the snow—until the chain finally snapped! It was unbelievable to watch. We had several camera angles of the action, and even added music to the video. Our fans loved it. More than 500,000 people watched the video on our channel, and it was viewed more than four million times on YouTube overall. That video put us on the social media map, and it was really a turning point in our growth as a company.

As crazy as it might sound, that video really helped launch our company. And once DieselSellerz was established on social media, its popularity exploded. Looking back now, it seems like it almost happened overnight, but we put in a lot of blood, sweat, and grease to make it happen. Once we started rebuilding more trucks and filming other crazy videos for YouTube and Facebook, we had tens of thousands of people viewing our channels and pages every month. Fortunately, we already had a plan in place to profit from our newfound popularity.

Sparks Motors, my original company, takes care of the actual mechanical work and builds the trucks. From engine work to engineering to paint and body repair, we've become a one-stop shop that rivals any garage in America. We buy and rebuild trucks of our own, and we're hired to do custom work for a handful of select customers every year, including a few famous ones.

DieselSellerz.com is an online marketplace we launched where people can buy and sell their trucks. We act more as a broker for private owners—it's like the world's largest Craigslist for diesel trucks—and sometimes we sell trucks there, too. Diesel Power Gear is our lifestyle brand, and dieselpowergear.com is where we sell T-shirts, apparel, and a ton of other merchandise. People can buy truck parts, lights, and other accessories, including Patriot Tires, which is our very own line of rubber treads. We've also launched redneckanything.com, where customers can buy products from other companies we have relationships with, such as Browning and Black Rhino tools.

A few months before we posted the video of the tug-of-war in the snow, I noticed that several companies were selling T-shirts and other apparel on websites that were geared toward people who drove diesel trucks. Owning a diesel truck is more of a lifestyle than a hobby for a lot of owners, and I figured we might be able to make some money by designing T-shirts and launching a website of our own.

I hired a Web designer off the Internet and I paid another guy to come up with a T-shirt design for our company. We put

"Rollin' Coal" on our first shirt with a pair of smokestacks. If you don't know—but I'm sure most of you do—"Rollin' Coal" refers to the practice of modifying engines and removing emissions controls to belch black smoke from a truck. It's a popular practice at truck pulls and monster truck events. Some guys even like to do it when they're riding down the highway. (Some dudes jokingly refer to the smoke as "Prius Repellent.") We're neither condemning nor condoning it. We don't do it, and we certainly don't promote tampering with emissions control systems because it's illegal in some states. But back then, "Rollin' Coal" was popular among diesel truck owners, and we used the reference to help promote our T-shirts, hoodies, and hats.

I'll tell you one thing: we knocked it out of the park with our first T-shirt. The week after we received our initial design, I ordered $15,000 worth of T-shirts and other apparel. The orders came in like crazy once we advertised them, and then Diesel Dave, my mom, and me spent many nights in our office stuffing T-shirts and hoodies into manila envelopes. We figured out the cheapest way to ship the merchandise was by using one-rate envelopes from the U.S. Postal Service. The only problem: the envelopes weren't really designed to hold hoodies and sweatshirts. So we practically ripped the envelopes apart and taped them back together again to save a couple of dollars. Hey, back then, every single dollar counted!

As long as we had the T-shirts in stock, they were selling like hotcakes on our website. By the beginning of 2013, I'd decided that we needed to launch a separate company to handle our merchandising. Diesel Dave and I were spending most of our time on rebuilds, finding parts, and helping the guys in the shop, and we couldn't be stuffing envelopes every night. So in March 2013, we launched Diesel Power Gear, which sold everything from T-shirts to hats to sweatshirts to bumper stickers. (Now we even sell truck parts like wheels, tires, grilles, lights, and bumpers, along with accessories such as bottle openers, beard kits, wallets, sunglasses, and just about anything else you'd want. Well, except for razors.)

By then, we'd moved from a small outbuilding on the Rockwell lot, which didn't even have a garage, to a 3,000-square-foot warehouse that had one entrance. Diesel Dave actually lived in that building (he'll tell you more about that below), but we needed more office space and a much bigger garage. We'd opened a separate marketing office, and I really wanted to have them in the same location to consolidate our overhead costs and merge operations.

After a few weeks of searching, I found what I believed was the perfect location—or at least pretty close to it. It was a shuttered frozen pizza distribution center in North Salt Lake City, and was a much larger metal building with three bay doors. The only problem: there were freezers inside that took up most of the floor space. For the building to be functional, the freezers had to go. I told the landlord that we'd remove the freezers if he'd give us a break on the rent.

We thought it would be easy to tear them down, but it wasn't. In fact, it was downright impossible. We couldn't get the freezers out the doors—I'd had Diesel Dave do the premeasurements—so we had to cut them in half. Worse, I'd counted on saving the freezers and selling them to repurpose the building like we needed it, but nobody was interested in buying them once they saw that they were cut in half. So instead of selling the freezers for $20,000 like I'd hoped, we used the six-inch panels to build a paint booth and a fence in the back. How's that for recycling?

We ended up staying in the pizza warehouse for about ten months. To be honest, the landlord asked us to leave because our one-year lease was running out and there were truck parts scattered all over the parking lot. We ended up leasing a corner of a trucking company's facility for three or four months, while I searched for another place for us to go. In June 2014, we moved to a warehouse in an industrial park in Woods Cross, Utah, and our marketing office was right next door. The warehouse was a former fiberglass production plant. It had two bay doors, but the shop and warehouse were too small. I had to find a facility that was much bigger for our rapidly expanding operation.

Fortunately, I found the perfect place right around the corner. When I first showed the building to Diesel Dave, he probably thought I was nuts. It was a 26,000-square-foot factory that was about to be condemned because it had been vacant for so long. It had been used as a sewing plant, and welding shop, and had several other uses over many decades. But there was a separate office, warehouse, and shop, and they were all together in the same three-and-a-half-acre facility. I negotiated an $8,000 monthly lease payment with the owner—after I agreed to clean out the mess inside. Over three months, we hauled off about 500 tons of trash out of the building. Then I took out a $250,000 small business loan and repurposed the factory to how we needed it to be. We put a retail space and offices in the front, shop and warehouse in the back, paint booth on the side, and parking lot in the rear. Even better: there is a private airport behind us, which helped facilitate my new hobby (more on that later). Plus, it has one of the most beautiful views you'll find anywhere with the Wasatch Range within plain sight out our back doors.

In July 2015, DieselSellerz moved into its new headquarters. Eventually, I was able to buy the factory for $600,000, and it's probably worth more than $2 million today. It's one of the best investments I've ever made. The facility has allowed us to expand our operations into some things we could have never imagined doing.

DIESEL DAVE: After we sold the Dodge Ram Mega Cab truck and the trade-in from our initial conversion, we bought a used Land Rover Discovery at auction for $4,500. Heavy D used it as his personal vehicle for a while, but then we decided to do something ambitious with it. We wanted to turn it into an off-road, four-wheeling machine!

We found a Land Rover diesel engine on the Internet and stuffed it into the Discovery. It was the first diesel conversion we did. We gave the truck a four-inch lift, new wheels and tires, and a custom bumper. We spent $4,500 on the engine and probably another $5,000 on other parts and customizations, bringing our total investment to about $14,000.

Once we were finished, and the Discovery was up and running, we advertised it on our Diesel Trucks For Sale page on Facebook. People went nuts over it. They'd never seen a souped-up Land Rover Discovery like ours. In fact, the owner of the Land Rover dealership in Las Vegas ended up buying the Discovery for $25,000, netting us an $11,000 profit. We used that money to rehabilitate the frozen pizza facility.

When we started doing more conversions, we started posting photos and videos to our social media accounts. More and more people started visiting our channels and pages. Then some representatives from Fusion Bumper called us and asked us if we wanted a free bumper to put on a truck. Additional sponsors like Spyder lights and FASS Fuel Systems eventually came on board, and we figured out we could add about $20,000 in upgrades to our builds—without spending a penny of our own money! The generosity of our sponsors and the partnerships we built with them really helped us produce some badass trucks that caught people's attention.

As Heavy D mentioned earlier, I actually lived in the pizza warehouse for a while. Honestly, it was a massive upgrade from my previous homes—the small outbuilding on the Rockwell lot and the 3,000-square-foot warehouse in the industrial park. When I slept at the Rockwell building, which was more like a trailer, it didn't even have a shower. I had to use the water hose at another outbuilding to bathe. I had the stench of almost being homeless; I smelled more like a shop. Hey, when you've slept in a hammock in the Amazon rain forest for weeks at a time, simply having a roof over your head seems like a luxury.

> *Hey, when you've slept in a hammock in the Amazon rain forest for weeks at a time, simply having a roof over your head seems like a luxury.*

Since I didn't have a shower or hot water, I rarely shaved and just let my beard grow. I'd had some pretty good ones in the past, including the time when I ran a marathon at the Great Wall of China. I probably looked like Forrest Gump running through the Chinese countryside. Heavy D kept telling me to shave because I looked like a bum. Somehow it went the other way, though, and he was able to grow one that was almost as good as mine. Then it kind of became a thing around the shop, in which everyone was trying to grow a beard. We tried to find out who wasn't man enough to grow one, and then we'd start making fun of them. I guess when all of this comes to an end—and it will end one day—our beards will give us an easy way to go back undercover. All we'll have to do is shave and it's likely no one will recognize us.

DIESEL HANDBOOK LESSON NO. 4
THE ART OF NEGOTIATION

After searching far and wide for the diesel truck of your dreams, you're finally ready to ditch your gasser for a set of monster wheels that are more reflective of your inner redneck.

Unfortunately, buying a new truck is like the last frontier of the wild, wild West. It's wheeling and dealing, and you have to be careful that an experienced salesman doesn't take advantage of you.

Here are some tips to know as you head into the negotiating process for your new truck:

1. Do your homework.

Once you determine which truck best fits your needs, whether it's an off-road vehicle, everyday driver, or a truck to tow, do enough research to figure out which trucks might be the best deals.

Use websites like *Kelley Blue Book* (kbb.com), Edmunds (edmunds.com), and TrueCar (truecar.com) to determine the appropriate retail and wholesale prices for a truck with mileage, condition, and options similar to the one you're considering.

By using those websites, you'll probably find several

trucks in your area that are similar in model, mileage, and condition. It's much easier to negotiate when you have a few options rather than one! And don't be afraid to look at trucks from outside your immediate area. You'd be surprised how many vehicles we've bought from faraway places, like California and Texas. It's never too far to go for the perfect truck!

2. Set a budget.

It's really important to know how much you can responsibly spend on a truck before you go shopping. You don't want to be driving a late-model Cummins and eating ramen noodles every night because you paid too much for your new truck! Be responsible about setting a budget and sticking to it. There are some great online affordability calculators that are easy to use.

It's important to remember that the sticker price of a truck is only the beginning of what you're going to spend. You also have to take into account insurance, fuel costs, regular mainte-nance like oil changes and tires, potential repairs, and annual registration and tag fees.

A good rule of thumb is to spend about 10 to 20 percent of your monthly income on a vehicle. If you don't have a lot of disposable income on hand, stick to the lower end. Most im-portant, don't let anyone talk you into buying something you can't afford. You don't want to be truck poor!

3. Secure financing in advance.

If you can secure financing in advance and walk into a dealership with a check in hand, it eliminates a lot of the drama and frustration that come with buying a new truck. If you're buying a used truck from an individual, they're going to be more willing to negotiate on the price if they don't have to wait for you to secure financing from a bank. Plus, if you really like a truck, you don't want somebody to swoop in and swipe it from under you while you're trying to come up with the money.

Of course, a dealership is probably going to try to pressure you into using one of their financing companies, because that's what they get paid to do. It's okay to talk to the dealership about financing because it might have lower interest rates than what you've already secured. Shop for the lowest rate and do what's best for you!

4. Don't get emotional.

Like I said earlier, it's best to have more than one option. It keeps you from getting too emotional about buying one truck. Even if you really like a truck, try to keep your head and don't get too excited. If you tell the seller it's the nicest truck you've ever seen and you never thought you'd be able to own a truck this nice in all of your life, well, now he's got you by the you-know-what!

Don't become too emotionally attached. If the salesman asks you if you want to take the truck home for an overnight test drive, politely decline his offer. Chances are you're only going to want to keep it (after you probably sleep in it), even if it's not the right truck for you.

It's important to be deliberate and disciplined in the buying process. Don't buy the first truck you see—shop around. There are plenty of fish in the diesel sea!

5. Don't negotiate.

Okay, if you've finally settled on the truck that's best for you, your financing is in place, and you've done the math and figured out you can afford the truck, it's time to start the negotiating process. Only you're not going to negotiate. Yeah, you heard me right.

Make the seller or salesman an offer and tell him that's the bottom line. Don't completely lowball the guy, because he won't take you seriously. Make him a fair, educated offer and tell him you're willing to buy the truck for that much and no more.

If you're dealing with a dealership, figure out the average retail price for similar trucks in the area and offer him 10–15 percent less. If the truck has problems you think you're going to have to eventually repair, offer him less. If you're dealing with an individual seller, you can probably offer him closer to the wholesale (or trade-in) price.

If the seller doesn't immediately accept your offer, give him your phone number and tell him you're very interested at the price you offered. Don't negotiate with him, and walk out the door.

6. Follow up with the seller.

After a couple of nights of restless sleep, in which you probably dreamed about your truck climbing rocks in Moab, check to see if the truck is still available. If it's still for sale, chances are he or she has probably already called you back.

But if they haven't, call them and let them know that you're still very interested in the truck and the price you offered. Tell them, if they want to sell it at that price, you can be there by the end of the day to close the deal. This tactic works especially well at the end of the month, when salespersons are under a lot of pressure to reach their quotas. Just remember: you're the one in charge and it's your money!

-*Heavy D*

CHAPTER SEVEN
SMOKIN' HOT WIVES

DIESEL DAVE: Do you know how you figure out if somebody's really your best friend? You live with him and his newlywed wife for five years—or you drive 6,000 miles on a school bus with him and six other dudes to Costa Rica and still talk to him afterward.

Shortly after Heavy D and his wife, Ashley, had their first child in 2011, he called me and asked me if I'd babysit his daughter so they could go on a date. I love kids and didn't have anything going on, so I agreed to do it. Well, I ended up moving in with Dave and Ashley shortly thereafter and lived with them for the next five years. Hey, their house was much more comfortable than where I had been living, which was a small room in our shop.

Living with Heavy D and Ashley was really an interesting

dynamic, and I don't think a lot of people could do it. But that's why they call us the Diesel Brothers. We're more family than best friends or business partners.

I still eat Thanksgiving dinner and celebrate Christmas with them every year. I dress up as Santa Claus for their kids and love doing it. As a result, Dave's kids and his nieces and nephews still believe in a very ugly Santa Claus. I even had to convince his daughter Charley that the real Santa Claus is my cousin!

> *But that's why they call us the Diesel Brothers. We're more family than best friends or business partners.*

When I lived with Heavy D, we'd carpool to work every morning. I think that was his way of making sure I was never late, because I rode to work with the boss. We'd get up early and work late, and then we'd get up and do it all over again the next day. Somehow, we never got tired of each other and never irritated one another, and I think that's the true sign of friendship.

After living with them for nearly five years, I started making plans to move out in 2015. I searched for a house to buy, and I was also looking for someone I might be able to settle down and start a family of my own with. I purchased my first house, but then I continued living in Heavy D's basement while I remodeled it (just like a truck, right?). Once I finished remodeling the upstairs, I moved into the house with my two hound dogs.

On May 16, 2015, I met the woman who would become my wife. That night, I went to see an Alan Jackson concert with a buddy of mine. We had just returned from a cruise to Jamaica, and I came back with braided hair and a braided beard. I was wearing nothing but overalls, and I know I looked cool. We were sitting in the back of my buddy's truck with a box of ducklings when a group of girls walked up. (And you thought puppies were chick magnets!) I thought one of the girls was smokin' hot, but I didn't think I stood a chance with her, because she wouldn't pay any attention to me. Even when we gave them a ride home after the concert, she didn't say much to me.

A couple of weeks later, the girl and one of her friends came to our shop, and I seized the moment. I wasn't going to let her slip out of my fingers again. I asked Deseri Huskinson out that day, and I ended up taking her to a pond to go fishing. We went dancing on another date, and we started spending a lot of time together. I couldn't let her out of my sight.

On my thirty-second birthday, in June 2016, Deseri asked me what I wanted for my birthday. I told her I wanted her forever, and fortunately she gave it to me. We made plans to get married in Italy, but there were problems with the paperwork. Instead, we were married in Las Vegas on July 4, 2016, and we honeymooned in Venice, Italy.

I really wanted to get married on the Fourth of July. I love our country so much, plus I knew there would be fireworks on our anniversary every year.

I really wanted to get married on the Fourth of July. I love our country so much, plus I knew there would be fireworks on our anniversary every year.

On January 12, 2017, Deseri gave birth to our daughter,

Saylor Fé Kiley. *Fé* means faith in Portuguese, and it's also Deseri's grandmother's name. Having a child was an absolute life changer for me. Once you have a daughter, you really start looking at your life and what you're doing completely different. In the span of about one year, I went from living in my best friend's basement, working as a mechanic, and not having much desire to do anything else to buying a house, getting married, and having a baby. That's a lifestyle change, brother.

Ironically, Tyson Ruth, one of our young mechanics and a good friend, is living in my basement now. It's like I have my own Diesel Dave living with me. My life has really come full circle.

HEAVY D: Now, you guys understand how great of a woman my wife, the former Ashley Bennett, really is to me. Not only did she put up with me after we were married, but she allowed my best friend to move into our house only a year after we were married. I don't think a bearded, jort-wearing, boot-stomping mechanic is what she had in mind for a nanny! But Ashley was absolutely fantastic and loved sharing our home with Diesel Dave.

I met Ashley at church in July 2009. At the time, her boyfriend from high school had just left for his LDS mission. To be honest, that's kind of how it works in the Mormon culture. You wait for a cute girl's boyfriend to leave for his mission and then make your move. Her boyfriend left on a Wednesday, and I called her on Sunday. Hey, I've never been known for my patience.

To Ashley's credit, she was pretty reluctant and wouldn't have anything to do with me. After several weeks of me pestering her, though, she finally agreed to go on a date with me. I guess my good looks and charm finally won her over. We fell in love and the rest is history. Seven years later, I'm still stunned she agreed to go out with me. I definitely out-punted my coverage, if you know what I mean.

We were engaged in June 2010 and were married at the Salt Lake temple on August 9, 2010. Before we were married, Diesel Dave and I, along with four of our friends, took a bachelors' trip back to Riberalta, Bolivia, which is where I did my LDS mission. We rented a Jeep and drove it as far into the jungle as we could go. Of course, we blew up the Jeep and had to catch a plane back to the city. As a result, our return to Salt Lake City kept getting delayed, and Ashley was worried that I wasn't going to make it back in time for our wedding. Fortunately, I did get back in time, and I'll never forget seeing Ashley in her white wedding dress. On our first Christmas together, Ashley gave me a Greater Swiss Mountain Dog we named Saint, and he became a wonderful pet.

Ashley and I didn't wait very long to start a family. I can't say it was planned, but it just kind of happened. Our daughter Charley was born in October 2011. It was the best day of our lives, and I've never seen Ashley so happy. It wasn't long after Charley's birth that we also picked up a roommate—Diesel Dave! As he told you, he came over to babysit Charley one night and kind of never left. It was convenient to have him there. He loved watching Charley, and we both trusted him with our daughter. It sure beat having a stranger come into our home to care for her.

In our first house, Diesel Dave's bedroom was right across the hall from our room. He was literally like ten feet away from my bedroom! In our second house, Dave lived in the basement, so Ashley and I had a little more privacy. Honestly, it really seemed kind of natural for him to be living with us. Diesel Dave has been around since my little girl was born, and Charley has always referred to him as Daddy No. 2. Our son, Beau, was born in May 2015, and then it was really good to have Dave around the house to help with two infants. Ashley was pregnant with our third child in 2017.

When Dave lived with us, he had a very unique way of lying low. I can honestly say I never got tired of him being there, and I never once heard Ashley say, "Man, this guy needs to get out of my space." He's so laid-back and doesn't need anything. Most of the time, it's like he wasn't even there. Plus, he helped take out the trash, cut the grass, and did other maintenance around the house. But the best part was that Diesel Dave loved being around our kids. It's kind of the way Dave is; he's always looking for a way to help others. He'll meet a stranger and ten minutes later he's committed to helping them move or doing whatever they need.

He'll meet a stranger and ten minutes later he's committed to helping them move or doing whatever they need.

Marrying Ashley and having a family with her has been

the greatest joy of my life. She's an unbelievable mother to our kids, and she really keeps our house in order. Once we agreed to do the reality TV show, I started working crazy hours. Ashley is one of the most patient and understanding women that you'll meet. She's really helped me become more grounded. In the past, I was a last-minute planner and wasn't very organized. If we were going on vacation, I wouldn't plan it until maybe a week in advance. If I was sitting at home on a weekend, and I was bored or got a wild hair, we'd jump on a plane and fly to go skiing in Jackson Hole, Wyoming, or we'd fly to Los Angeles to go to Disneyland. We can't do that anymore with kids. We still have a great time together, but instead of flying to California or Hawaii, we'll take the kids up into the mountains or to the lake for a day. It's what we absolutely love to do, as long as we're all together.

About two years after Ashley and I were married, we planned a trip to Costa Rica. Well, Dave and I planned a crazy road trip with a group of our buddies, and then Ashley and the other wives flew to Costa Rica to meet us at a resort. We called it the "Great Bus Adventure." We bought a used yellow bus from a school district in eastern Utah and started driving south. I'd been away on business, so they picked me up in Texas. Then we picked up a few more friends in Mexico City. Jackknife Jim Anderson and Van Oakes, who still work with us today, were on the trip, along with seven other guys. We were crammed onto the bus together for eleven days, and it's a trip that none of us will ever forget. We threw a gun in a garbage can at the

Mexican border, and bathed in swimming holes, waterfalls, and rivers along the way. Once we reached Costa Rica, we gave the bus away and flew back to Salt Lake City with our wives.

Those are the kind of memories Diesel Dave and I will remember forever. We've been making them together for more than a decade, and now we look forward to making many more with our wives and children. I'm telling you: there's not a job in the world better than working with your best friend.

I'm telling you: there's not a job in the world better than working with your best friend.

It's nice to go to work every day with a smile on your face, and then go home to your wife and kids when you're still in a good mood. It makes all the difference in the world.

CHAPTER EIGHT
THE GIVEAWAY

HEAVY D: Some of the greatest companies in the world survived only after their founders took huge risks in trying to keep them afloat. When FedEx (then Federal Express) was on the verge of collapse in the early 1970s, founding CEO Fred Smith took the company's last $5,000 and went to Las Vegas, where he gambled it in blackjack. He walked away that weekend with $32,000, giving FedEx enough money to fuel its planes for deliveries for another week. Today, FedEx does more than $50 billion in annual revenue. When the U.S. economy collapsed in 2008, new automobile company Tesla was unable to deliver its first cars as promised, so founder Elon Musk took his last $35 million and dumped it into his company. Tesla survived and is worth more than $2.5 billion today. Talk about doubling down!

We faced the same kind of dilemma—albeit on a much smaller scale—as a company in 2013. By then we were beginning to realize what we were. We were building these crazy trucks and people were going wild about them. The trucks were bringing a lot more traffic to our social media channels and websites, which really increased our T-shirt and apparel sales. But we were trying to figure out a way to expand our company even more and make it even more profitable.

In April 2013, we posted a photograph of three trucks—a Chevrolet, Dodge, and Ford—and asked our fans which truck they'd choose if they could have one. One of the commenters on our Facebook page said, "Hey, you guys should really think about giving away one of your trucks in a contest." The more we thought about it, the more sense it made. People were giving away trucks, but they were usually stock and straight off a car lot. There wasn't anything really special about them. Conversely, we wanted to give away somebody's dream truck. We wanted to give them a ride that would knock them on their ass.

> *We wanted to give them a ride that would knock them on their ass.*

In the end, we decided, why not? It was going to be a hell of a lot of fun to build the truck and give it away, and hopefully the contest would bring a lot more attention to our company and traffic to our websites.

We figured out that if we developed a sweepstakes built around T-shirt and apparel sales, it might make enough money to cover the costs of the truck, and maybe even make us some additional revenue. Our tremendous sponsors were already supplying us with enough parts and services to rebuild the trucks like we wanted, so we'd really only have to cover the costs of the bones of the truck and the manpower to convert it into a badass ride. You should have seen Redbeard's face when I told him we were going to give away a truck!

We hired random.org, an online company that people use to stage lotteries, sweepstakes, and contests, to help us conduct our giveaway. The basic premise was pretty simple: Whenever someone purchased a T-shirt or other apparel from our website, they received a game chip, which entered them into our contest. If they purchased five T-shirts, for instance, they received five entries into our giveaway. You didn't have to actually purchase something to be included in the drawing; you could also write us a letter explaining why you deserved to win the truck. Some people wondered why we didn't have an online link to be registered, but we didn't think that would capture the essence of what owning a diesel is about. We thought you should have to do a little bit of work and heavy lifting to win a diesel truck. We received so many letters from people telling us about how they were the greatest diesel enthusiasts. Plus, we saw some really cool photos of their trucks.

By hiring random.org, we took choosing the winner out of our hands. It made the contest legitimate and objective because it was a third-party company that had absolutely no affiliation to us. It also took human error out of the process. Once all the names were entered in the raffle through retail purchases or letters we received, a computer randomly chose a winner and that was that.

While it was an exciting proposition, it was also terrifying as hell because all of the money we made from T-shirt sales the previous two years was going to be spent on buying the truck we were going to give away. We ended up buying a 2012 Dodge Ram 2500 SLT for $40,000. We didn't really choose the truck—our fans did. We did online polls and asked them what kind of truck they wanted us to give away, and there are a lot of Dodge fans out there. Honestly, our fans built the truck from the ground up. They wanted a black truck, so we bought a black truck. They wanted a six- to eight-inch lift, and they wanted a Cummins engine, which was an easy choice.

In reality, picking a Dodge was the best choice for us because there are so many parts and options available for them. More than anything, we wanted to build a functional truck. We wanted to give somebody a truck they could drive to work and use on the weekends. But it was still going to be kick-ass. The real magic was going to happen under the hood with the 6.7-liter Cummins diesel engine. The new trucks come with diesel particulate filters (DPFs) and exhaust gas recirculation systems. They cut down on emissions, but it makes it difficult to build a lot of power. We wanted to build a 650-horsepower engine with a DPF filter still on it. We didn't want it to be blowing smoke and ticking off other drivers. We wanted a nice, clean running truck that was still very powerful, and that's what we were going to try to build.

Well, after we announced the giveaway contest in late April 2013 on our social media channels, our fans were blown away, to say the least. In the first two days after we announced the contest, we probably did $50,000 to $60,000 in retail sales. It was nuts. In only forty-eight hours, we basically covered the cost of buying the truck and the labor it would take to rebuild it like we wanted. After the initial surge, excitement kind of waned over the next couple of months, and we probably did $15,000 to $20,000 in retail sales each month. But as we got closer to the August 1 deadline for the contest, sales really skyrocketed again. When it was all said and done, we ended up doing close to $350,000 in retail sales during the six-month contest. After we paid for the truck, labor, and the cost of the apparel that everyone purchased, we probably made $50,000 to $60,000 in profit.

It worked out, but it was a huge gamble because we didn't know if we were going to end up being able to pay for the truck and everything else. All of the work we'd done in 2011 and 2012 was on the line if the giveaway wasn't a success. If we hadn't made enough money to cover our costs, it would have wiped us out and we probably wouldn't be here today.

If we hadn't made enough money to cover our costs, it would have wiped us out and we probably wouldn't be here today.

We would have been forced to start from scratch again. We'd started over before, like when our landscaping company folded, but it would have been much more difficult this time because I had a family to feed.

DIESEL DAVE: The coolest part about the giveaways for me is that I get to personally give the trucks to the winners and take them to a steak dinner.

Our first winner is a guy that I'll never forget. Ashton Barton of Sedalia, Missouri, won Built Diesel 1 on September 5, 2013. He was a nineteen-year-old guy who grew up in a single-parent home. His mother did a great job of raising him, but they didn't have much money and he really wanted a diesel truck. His mother had made a lot of sacrifices while raising him, and he'd worked hard for everything he had. He couldn't afford a diesel truck so winning one from us was a dream come true for him. I couldn't have handpicked a better winner for our first contest.

Ashton won a sweet ride, that's for sure. We ended up giving his truck a six-inch Pro Comp long arm lift kit with ES 9000 shocks. We also put 37-inch Pro Comp mud terrain extreme tires on his truck, with black 20x12 LGR wheels. The wheels and tires were pretty sweet. One of my favorite parts about the rebuild was putting Fusion bumpers on the front and back of the Ram 2500. We covered them in Scorpion bedliner, which we also put all around the base of the truck to protect it from rock chips. AMP Research also provided us with power steps to make it easier for Ashton to climb in and out of his truck and bed, since it was sitting so high. There was also a Smitty-bilt bed cover, Monster hooks, and a Smittybilt 12,000-pound winch on the front. There were plenty of Rigid lights and G2 axle and gear differential covers underneath. What more could a guy want?

But the real jewel was under the hood. Industrial Injections of Salt Lake City gave us a 64mm Silver Bullet Turbo with matching injectors. The engine was capable of producing about 700 horsepower without getting hot. By the time our guys were done, the CP3 injection pumps and FASS fuel system were pumping about 150 gallons per hour. We replaced the stock transmission with an ATS Stage 3 transmission, which would be able to adequately keep up with the power.

The interior of the truck was just as sweet. Since it was an SLT and already pretty nice, we didn't have to do a lot. But we added more than a few luxuries. We covered the cloth seats in new leather from leatherseats.com, and Frequency Mobile Innovations installed a JVC DVD player in the dash, which controlled XM radio, navigation, and everything else. We tinted the windows at 20 percent to make the interior nice and cool, and added Wade floor mats to keep the carpet clean. The icing on the cake was an H&S performance tuner, which made the truck run and drive perfectly. When you put everything together, there was probably $30,000 to $40,000 in upgrades. The truck was worth roughly $75,000 to $80,000 overall, which would have put it among the Rolls-Royces of trucks.

Ashton, like all of our future winners, had to decide whether he was going to keep the truck and pay the sales tax and income taxes that came with winning it. Or he could sell the truck and use the money to pay the taxes for the income he earned by selling it, but then still have enough money in his pocket to buy a truck that wasn't as nice. I don't think it was much of a dilemma for him. He decided to keep the truck and still has it.

When Ashton's name was selected as the winner, we flew him to Salt Lake City. We drove his new truck to the airport and met him outside baggage claim. When he climbed behind the steering wheel for the first time, he was completely blown away. We were really happy he won it because it was obviously going to dramatically change his life. We posted a video of him receiving and driving the truck, which silenced a few of our critics. I think some people out there thought the contest might be a scam because they couldn't believe we were really going to give away a $75,000 truck. But I think seeing Ashton so happy gave us some legitimacy.

By the end of the contest, our social media following had increased dramatically. We probably had close to 400,000 followers on Facebook and nearly twice that many on Instagram. We were posting some crazy videos and giving people updates on our trucks. To be honest, I think people were more interested in what we were going to do next than our products. We'd kind of come out of nowhere and people were eager to see the crazy stuff that was happening in our shop.

After that first giveaway, I started pushing Heavy D if I could be the guy that went out and appeared on the videos. I was comfortable being in front of cameras and people seemed to like my jokes, even if most of them were pretty corny. Fortunately for me, Heavy D gave me the freedom to do it. I'm all about sharing fun stuff on social media, and there are a lot of people out there who like to have as much fun as us. Well, maybe not quite as much fun. It wouldn't be very long before Heavy D realized how much of a risk came with putting a video camera in my hands.

It wouldn't be very long before Heavy D realized how much of a risk came with putting a video camera in my hands.

When we gave away another truck about four months later in our Built Diesel 2 contest, we decided to take the truck to the winner and surprise him. As luck would have it, Jason Ruark of Salisbury, Maryland, won a 2013 Ford F-250 Super Duty. He lived not too far from where Heavy D was born, but it was a long way from Salt Lake City! We picked the winner on New Year's Day 2014, but then we kept Jason's identity secret until we finished the final upgrades and delivered his truck about two months later.

Since we were going to have to drive more than 2,000 miles through ten states over three days, we decided to make it an epic road trip that we would never forget. We had a live video feed of our trip on our website, and we posted updates and videos of our progress on social media. Along the way, we left prizes and met fans at various stops. We left one-hundred-dollar bills under bottles of windshield wiper fluid in gas stations and told fans to meet us at rest stops and other places for free T-shirts and other apparel. It was a blast and we met so many great people.

Once we reached Bentonville, Arkansas, our road trip to Maryland went into overdrive, to say the least. We told people to meet us in an open field, and we were expecting maybe ten or twenty people to be there. But when we arrived at the field, there were probably 200 people and 100 trucks. It was nuts. It was like Dieselpalooza.

But when we arrived at the field, there were probably 200 people and 100 trucks. It was nuts. It was like Dieselpalooza.

Guys were doing donuts and spinning out in their trucks, and then somebody drove a blue Toyota Prius into the field. Well, that's like dropping a truckload of New York strip steaks into an alligator farm. The next thing we knew, guys were smashing the Prius with cinder blocks and sledgehammers. Then they hooked steel chains to six trucks and pulled the Prius apart! There wasn't a salvageable part left on that hybrid by the time they were done. (Not that you'd want a part off a Prius!) We thought our trip to Bentonville was only going to be a pit stop, but we ended up staying in that field all night. It was so much fun.

We met so many great diesel fanatics on the road. A few guys even took us to dinner in Indianapolis. When we finally reached the Maryland coast, we arrived at Jason's house in the middle of a snowstorm. We were happy to see a Ford truck sitting in his driveway. We were excited to learn he was a Ford guy because he would really appreciate what we were about to give him.

When Jason answered the door, he couldn't believe Heavy D and I were standing on his front porch. The truck he won was beautiful. We put an eight-inch lift on the F-250 Super Duty, painted it white, and wrapped the top in black. It had 20-inch wheels with 38-inch Toyo tires, Fusion bumpers, Rigid light bar and reverse lights, and a Lariat leather package in the interior. It was so plush and sweet. With added turbo and a FASS fuel system under the hood, the truck had about 575 horsepower. It was a mean ride. After dropping off Jason's truck, we realized we didn't have a truck to get us home! We hitched a ride to Washington, D.C., where we spent the night before flying home the next day.

As great as Built Diesel 2 ended up being for us, our Built Diesel 3 contest was even bigger and better. During a momentary lapse of judgment, we decided to give away three trucks to three winners—at the same time. The grand prize winner would get to choose one of three awesome trucks: 1997 Ford F-250 Power Stroke, 1994 Dodge Ram 3500 12-valve Cummins, and 2006 Chevy Duramax. The first runner-up would get to pick next, and then the second runner-up would get to have the truck that was left. It was a really cool contest and generated a ton of online traffic and sales for our websites. It was also a ton of work building three trucks at once.

On May 28, 2014, we announced the winners in order: Luke Kapelanczyk of Kellogg, Idaho; James Van Wingerden of Sunnyside, Washington; and Ryan Hutchinson of Folsom, California. Since Luke had the first choice among the trucks, we drove all three of them to Kellogg (with the Cummins pulling a trailer hauling the other two, of course). It was about a nine-hour drive from Salt Lake City to the Idaho panhandle.

Luke ended up choosing the Cummins, and he kept it for a short while before trading it for something else. (FYI: We don't get upset if someone sells or trades one of our trucks. They won the truck and it's their property. We want our trucks to be owned by people who can use and enjoy them.)

We want our trucks to be owned by people who can use and enjoy them.

The Cummins was one of our military tributes and was a very sweet truck.

James had the second choice, so we had to travel from Idaho to Sunnyside, Washington, which was only about three hours away and was a gorgeous drive. James picked the Duramax because he was a Chevrolet guy. He already owned a Chevy truck and added another horse to his stable. That left the Ford F-250 for Ryan, and it took us about eleven hours to drive from Washington to Folsom, which is outside Sacramento, California.

Ryan seemed to be the most excited among the three winners. He was a firefighter, and it felt good to give a badass truck to someone who put his life on the line for others. We have a lot of respect for police officers, firefighters, and first responders. They're heroes in our eyes, and we'll do anything we can do to help. The F-250 that Ryan won had a 7.3-liter Power Stroke engine and manual transmission. It drove like a tank, which is how trucks are supposed to ride. It was a solid, everyday truck, but there wasn't anything normal about it.

The Built Diesel 3 contest was a lot of work because we had to build three trucks. We obviously had a lot of money invested in the contest, but it all worked out in the end. Those two weeks we spent on the road for Built Diesel 2 and Built Diesel 3—and the countless hours we spent in the shop building those trucks—were worth it once we saw the smiles on the winners' faces.

DIESEL HANDBOOK LESSON NO. 5
TRUCK PRANKS

Like most things in life, the level of truck pranks largely depends on one's creativity, commitment, and, most important, cash flow. With enough time and money, you can do just about anything with somebody's truck. But there are also simple gags that you can pull off to shake things up.

Of course, I'm not condoning you doing anything that would permanently alter a truck or put anyone in a dangerous situation. This is only clean, old-fashioned fun, and we're hoping everyone gets a good laugh out of our pranks and practical jokes.

Here are eight gags that will have your buddies rolling in the street:

1. Magnetic bumper stickers

It's amazing what you can find on Amazon.com to decorate your buddies' bumpers. In about two minutes, I found the following magnetic bumper stickers: Pay Cuts for Cops, Warning: Cowboy Butts Drive Me Nuts, and I Love Dogs, Especially With Some BBQ Sauce. And then there's my personal favorite: Honk If You Have to Poop. Watch him roll down the highway as everyone honks at him!

If you have a buddy that's a Boston Red Sox fan, put a New

York Yankees bumper sticker on his truck. If he likes the Chicago Cubs, use the Chicago White Sox. If you have a friend who likes the San Francisco 49ers, put a Raiders sticker on his bumper. You can find something that will irritate your buddies for sure.

2. Broken window

This trick is going to require a little bit of work and a lot of caution. Go to a salvage yard and find the cheapest car window you can find. Then break it somewhere where you can easily sweep up the glass. Make sure you wear gloves and goggles, and be sure to leave part of the bottom of the window intact. That will come in handy later.

When your buddy is asleep at home or busy at work, get his truck keys and lower his driver's-side window. Then scatter the broken glass on the ground outside his truck and throw some inside on the floor mat as well. Place the bottom of the broken window where his window is supposed to go, and then wait for him to come out and see the shattered glass. He'll instantly think someone broke into his truck! Make sure he realizes it's a joke and doesn't call the police!

3. Colored wiper fluid

If you're going off-road with someone and know they'll be using their wiper fluid to clean the windshield, sneak a few drops of food coloring into the tank to give them a big surprise! Then, when the windshield gets dusty, watch his eyes bug out when he sees orange, red, blue, or green all over the glass.

4. Noisy brakes

If you're pretty knowledgeable about a truck's wiring, connect the brake lights to the horn. It's relatively easy and can be reversed in only a few minutes. When your buddy taps on the brakes of his truck, the horn will sound. Do it right before he drives downtown into traffic, and he'll really be annoyed with you! And so will everyone else on the streets!

5. The faux accident

When your friend is at work or he's at the grocery store, leave a note under his windshield wiper that says, "Sorry, I hit your truck while I was backing up. I have a sick child and need to get to the doctor's office. Call me when you have time, and we'll work out arrangements for payment. I don't have money, but maybe we can trade out for babysitting or yard work."

After reading that note, your buddy will undoubtedly spend the next thirty minutes looking for a scratch or dent on his truck, and he'll probably end up finding a ding that he's sure wasn't there before!

6. Wrap a truck

If you know your buddy is going to be at work or away from his truck for a few hours, cover his ride in carbon fiber wrap. This prank is going to cost you a little bit of money and it's going to take some time, but it's going to be hilarious and well worth the effort. You can buy vinyl wrap in any color on the Internet, including pink, and it doesn't damage the existing paint. Hey, if you don't want to spend the money, use plastic wrap or toilet paper.

7. Craigslist

If you have a friend who is very emotionally attached to his truck and thinks it's the sweetest ride to ever grace the highway, take a photo of it and advertise it on Craigslist or eBay. Even better: advertise it for a price that's a couple of thousand dollars below *Kelley Blue Book* value. That should really drum up interest in his truck! Make sure you add his phone number or email address to the ad, and then watch his smartphone blow up!

8. Hood ornaments

Believe me, there's nothing a Ford truck owner hates more than a Chevrolet, or a Dodge truck owner hates more than a Ford. If your friend drives a Chevy, buy a peel-and-stick Ford emblem off Amazon.com and apply it to his truck's hood or grille. If he owns a Dodge, use a Ford one. Trust me: it won't be on there for long. That's savage.

—Diesel Dave

CHAPTER NINE
REDBEARD & THE MUSCLE

HEAVY D: Throughout history, almost every successful person had a right-hand man (or woman) behind him or her. U.S. presidents have a vice president, and Super Bowl–winning coaches have coordinators and assistant coaches. NASCAR drivers have a crew chief and pit crew, and surgeons and doctors have nurses and other technicians working alongside them in the operating room. Think about it: What would Apple cofounder Steve Jobs have done without Steve Wozniak, and what would Rolling Stones frontman Mick Jagger have been without Keith Richards? There is always someone working in the shadows to help the guys and girls out front.

When I went about building my companies, I wanted to surround myself with people who were like-minded, honest and trustworthy, driven and committed, and who believed in my vision strongly enough to get in line and follow me. Although I had a lot of faith in my own skills and abilities, I sought to hire people who were more talented and smarter than me.

> Although I had a lot of faith in my own skills and abilities, I sought to hire people who were more talented and smarter than me.

More than anything, I wanted to surround myself with people who were good at things that I wasn't particularly good at doing. In the end, I knew they were only going to make me look good if I gave them the space and freedom to do their jobs and do what they do well.

I also wanted to hire people who would mesh with the culture and environment we were building. I had to find people who would fit in with my other employees and work well with them. We needed people who would share the same goals and values and who could fill in the gaps where needed. Anyone can have great ideas and talents, but if they can't share that information in ways that others can digest, they're not nearly as valuable. You can't hire people who are different from everyone else at your company. They'll stick out like a sore thumb and won't get along with everyone else. You'll end up spending too much time settling disagreements and disputes in the shop.

In addition to hiring people who are capable of doing their jobs, such as skilled mechanics, quality paint and body shop guys, and resourceful and personable salespeople, you have to find people who are committed and dedicated. Just because someone is qualified to do his or her job doesn't necessarily mean they'll do it. You have to find people who love what they're doing and are eager to learn and master their skills. I wanted creative people who could think outside the box and overachieve. I wanted to work with passionate, positive, organized, and conscientious people who took great pride in their work and cared about the product we would be producing.

Hiring Diesel Dave to work with me was a no-brainer. We were already close friends, and we'd worked together at my landscaping company and Rockwell Watches. He loved diesel trucks as much as I did, and I knew the guy was an absolutely relentless worker and was extremely loyal. Plus, I needed Diesel Dave around to tell jokes and keep people laughing. If you haven't figured it out yet, I'm one of the worst joke tellers in the entire state of Utah. No matter how hard I try, I'm just not very funny. My delivery is always off, and I always seem to get the punch lines wrong.

Diesel Dave is the Dave Chappelle of the diesel world. He makes the best jokes and delivers them exactly right.

Conversely, Diesel Dave is the Dave Chappelle of the diesel world. He makes the best jokes and delivers them exactly right.

Honestly, he could make Madonna laugh at a Donald Trump rally.

Once our partnership was in place, two of our most important hires at Sparks Motors and DieselSellerz.com were bringing The Muscle and Redbeard on board to help us. I recognized that both of them had tremendous skills we lacked. The Muscle can sell anything. He could sell ice to an Eskimo or sawdust to a lumber mill. The guy has an insane ability to connect with people and persuade them that they need what he's selling.

Redbeard, on the other hand, isn't so much a salesman as he is a numbers guy and chief financial officer. He has an innate ability to see the big picture and understand the larger consequences of our decisions. Most important, he likes to do what nobody else wants to do: he balances our books and keeps us within budget on our builds. Because of their abilities, The Muscle and Redbeard have been invaluable in helping our businesses grow to what they are today.

Now, you've probably seen The Muscle, whose real name is Keaton Hoskins, on the *Diesel Brothers* show. He's one of the main characters and one of our best friends. The Muscle loves God, his family, his country, diesel trucks, and football, probably in that order. He's a huge fan of the San Francisco 49ers and the Utah Utes. In fact, he's president of the local Colin Kaepernick fan club (I'm kidding; he couldn't stand the guy when he was the 49ers' quarterback).

The Muscle and Diesel Dave have known each other since the eighth grade. They grew up playing football and rugby together, but then they kind of lost touch after they went on their mission trips. When we first started our company, we'd bump into The Muscle at truck shows, races, and other events. He comes from a family of diesel fanatics and always loved driving and building diesel trucks. In 2013, The Muscle responded to one of our early Craigslist ads and then asked us to do a build for him. We rebuilt his single-wheeled Dodge 2500 into an all-black dually that was pretty sweet. I think it was really just a way for The Muscle to get his foot into the door with us.

In 2013, we hired The Muscle and put him in charge of finding parts and identifying potential sponsors for our builds. He's a very capable salesman because he's a good talker, and he's a great negotiator because he's persistent and stubborn. More than anything else, The Muscle is the epitome of an entrepreneur. At various times, he had ownership stakes in a fitness gym, dental office, and plastic surgery practice (fortunately, he wasn't working on clients' teeth or noses). Obviously, he's much more than big muscles; he's a great businessman and has brought a lot of valuable knowledge to our operation.

Like Diesel Dave, The Muscle came from a big family—he has three brothers and one sister—and like me he lost his father too early. His dad, Mark Hoskins, was an engineer in the aerospace industry and loved to talk to people. He was also famously stubborn and liked to debate; I think that's where Keaton probably gets his negotiating skills. The Muscle's dad encouraged his kids to always give 110 percent, and I know that's where he gets his passion and determination to achieve. Keaton's dad died after a long illness in 2008.

As his moniker suggests, The Muscle has been a personal fitness trainer for a very long time. He had an interest in bodybuilding since high school and has probably trained more than 2,500 people during the past decade. He helps people develop nutrition plans and exercise programs, and he coaches and encourages them along the way. He gets a lot of satisfaction out of helping people reach their fitness goals. Many of his clients compete in bodybuilding events around the country. The Muscle was a bodybuilder himself and his last competition was at the 2013 Complete Nutrition Bodybuilding Championships in Salt Lake City. He trained for that event for nearly a year and looked good; we think he's been eating junk food ever since.

While The Muscle is a fantastic businessman, friend, and employee, most important is that he's a great husband and father. Keaton and his wife, Jenny, have two beautiful daughters, Tea and Cali, who have him wrapped around their fingers. He loves taking his daughters sledding or snowmobiling and he even gets pedicures and manicures with them. While The Muscle might look like a rough-and-tough dude on the outside, he has a very soft spot in his heart for his little girls. He calls Cali, his younger daughter, "Goodness" because she reminds him of everything that is good in the world.

DIESEL DAVE: I've got to be honest: When Heavy D told me he was hiring Redbeard, I didn't know what to think. I'd always been a little frightened of redheads, especially after I watched Scut Farkus bully Ralphie Parker and his buddies in *A Christmas Story*. (And, of course, I had to find out if your tongue really sticks to a metal pole in the winter. Spoiler: It does!) Groundskeeper Willie from *The Simpsons* and the Chucky doll from *Child's Play* freaked me out when I was a kid, too. As far as I knew, every redhead had a short temper or mean streak and was a potential serial killer.

> As far as I knew, every redhead had a short temper or mean streak and was a potential serial killer.

The more I thought about it, though, the more sense it made for us to hire Redbeard when we did. We still didn't have a company mascot, and hiring him was probably cheaper than us paying licensing rights to use Yosemite Sam or Hagar the Horrible.

Jokes aside, Redbeard is a fantastic guy and a great friend. He is really smart when it comes to money, and it takes a lot of backbone, patience, and discipline to keep guys like us in line—and under budget.

Redbeard, or Josh Stuart, grew up in Roosevelt, Utah, which is a small town of about 4,000 people located 100 miles east of Salt Lake City. Roosevelt is located in the Uintah Basin, which was part of the Ute Indian reservation that opened to settlers in 1905. Redbeard graduated from Union High School and then studied economics at the University of Utah and Utah State. That's where his financial background comes from.

By the time we met Redbeard, he had already started and sold several businesses. He worked as a sales representative and trainer for a security company after college, going door-to-door in the summer selling security systems. Then he founded his own pest control company in Sandy, Utah, and sold it after turning it into a success in only three years. He went back to work as a sales manager for a security firm before starting an investment services company.

Although Redbeard found success at a relatively young age, I think he wanted an opportunity to literally let his hair grow. After a mutual friend recommended Redbeard to Heavy D as a potential moneyman, he joined Diesel Power Gear as chief financial officer and chief operating officer in October 2013.

Now I think Josh honestly believes his red beard is like Samson's hair, and it will lose its supernatural powers if he trims it.

He's been growing his Viking red beard ever since. Oddly enough, Josh didn't even know he had red-headed genes until he started growing a beard. Most of the hair on his head is sandy blond! Now I think Josh honestly believes his red beard is like Samson's hair, and it will lose its supernatural powers if he trims it.

Here's all you need to know about Redbeard: He worked the first six months with us for free to prove himself. He isn't a mechanic and doesn't know a lot about trucks. It just isn't his thing. But Redbeard is a fantastic marketing and financial guy, and he recognized that the future of our company was tremendous and it was a great opportunity for him to help us grow. He was the one that really pushed the use of social media and videos in the beginning. It was his foresight that really put our company in motion. He's also very resourceful. When he locked himself out of his office one time, he grabbed the nearest

Discovery Channel

A young Diesel Dave and his parakeet.

Author's Collection

Ready to get on the road.

Author's Collection

Heavy D loved bikes from a young age.
Author's Collection

Goofing around on
a mission.
Author's Collection

The magic school bus.
Author's Collection

Going to the chapel.
Author's Collection

Bringing good cheer to the Diesel clan.

Author's Collection

Hanging with Jay Leno!

Author's Collection

Heavy D working on the F650 build.
Discovery Channel

Chavis Fryer and Chet Ruth working on the El Camino build.
Discovery Channel

The F650 truck parked inside the garage before the build.
Discovery Channel

Diesel Dave shopping for a seventies outfit to wear in the El Camino video. *Discovery Channel*

Diesel Dave holding the winner's name during the live drawing for the giveaway. *Discovery Channel*

Keaton "The Muscle" Hoskins. *Discovery Channel*

Discovery Channel

The Diesel Brothers are ready for the Mud Bog ride in the back of their truck.

Discovery Channel

The guys taking a break from the heat in Diesel Dave's truck bed turned pool.

Discovery Channel

Getting back to work.

Discovery Channel

Diesel Dave and Steve working on the SnoCat build.

Discovery Channel

Diesel Dave and Redbeard preparing to sandblast the Holy Grail truck.
Discovery Channel

Horsing around.
Discovery Channel

Waterskiing? Wakeboarding? There is nothing this Denali can't do.

Discovery Channel

Heavy D shows the DieselSellerz crew his idea for the latest giveaway.

Discovery Channel

Nothing says fancy like Diesel Dave and The Muscle dressed to the nines, drinking champagne in front of an airplane and their top-of-the-line Denali. *Discovery Channel*

The DieselSellerz crew shoots giveaway video for the Mud Truck Giveaway.
Discovery Channel

Go-carts stand ready for the race to determine who will win the H1 Hummer.
Discovery Channel

The front of the Fail of the Year is in the shop.
Discovery Channel

Fail of the Year with Dave Sparks in the driver's seat.
Discovery Channel

The Truck Norris logo.
Discovery Channel

The Muscle picks up the Motoped.
Discovery Channel

The final Somersault truck build on the test day.
Discovery Channel

Selfie time!

Discovery Channel

The Mega RamRunner.

Discovery Channel

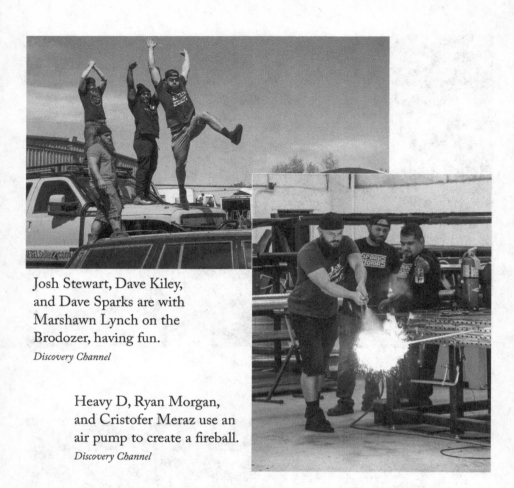

Josh Stewart, Dave Kiley, and Dave Sparks are with Marshawn Lynch on the Brodozer, having fun.
Discovery Channel

Heavy D, Ryan Morgan, and Cristofer Meraz use an air pump to create a fireball.
Discovery Channel

Fire in the hole!
Discovery Channel

power tool he could find, instead of finding a spare key or calling a locksmith. He happened to grab a Sawzall and proceeded to cut a very large hole in his office door. It kept getting bigger and bigger until he could reach in with his arm and unlock his door. Now he has a very big peephole in his office door!

Josh and his wife, April, have four beautiful children: Wolfgang, Rad, Soleil, and Luna (none of them are redheads). Now you know why Redbeard is often the one that comes up with the names for our trucks. When people say there's a greater woman behind every great man, they're talking about Josh and April. Redbeard loves the Los Angeles Dodgers (by marriage), hunting, MMA fighting, and billiards, and I think his proudest moment on *Diesel Brothers* occurred when he met Chuck Norris and realized he was also a redhead. So the next time you tell a redhead joke, just remember that Chuck Norris might overhear it!

With Redbeard and The Muscle on board, we had the top of our order in place. Now we had to find the utility men and support staff to make our companies smooth-running machines.

CHAPTER TEN
PRANKS

DIESEL DAVE: Who doesn't like to laugh? Practical jokes, hoaxes, tricks, capers, and pranks are what keep us laughing and living. Growing up, I learned that the family that laughs together stays together.

> *Growing up, I learned that the family that laughs together stays together.*

When I was a kid, I loved whoopee cushions, electric handshake buzzers, and bubble gum that turned your teeth black. I loved prank calls (Hello, Mr. Whitehead? Oh, sorry, wrong zit!), sending pizza delivery guys to my buddy's houses, and calling their dads and pretending to be the Internal Revenue Service (now, that's cold).

If you asked Heavy D, my wife, or any of my friends, they'd probably tell you that I never grew up. In a lot of ways, I'm still a kid. I love pranks and practical jokes, and I've tried to create a fun environment at Diesel Brothers to keep us all sane. Sure, we work hard and take a lot of pride in what we do, but what's the use in doing it if you're not having fun? Enjoying each other and laughing together should be the foundation of any relationship, and I think that's one of the reasons our crew is so close. It's why we're much more like family and friends than coworkers and employees.

Once Heavy D handed me control of our social media channels, I wanted to film the fun stuff we were doing behind the scenes to show our fans. Along with crazy driving stunts and stupid human tricks, I wanted to come up with some legendary pranks and practical jokes. When Heavy D finally loosened my reins, it was like giving a blank canvas to Picasso, an empty notebook to Hemingway, or a blank audiotape to Tupac. I was determined to try things that had never been attempted in the world of comedy and capture them on film for everyone to see.

Like anything else, my practical jokes started with baby steps. We filmed crazy ATV spinouts in the snow, diesel truck tug-of-wars, and tire burnout challenges. Before too long, though, I graduated to more challenging and dangerous stunts and practical jokes. We filmed me jumping over a Built Diesel truck that was running straight at me. I was actually attached to a bungee cord that was tied to an excavator bucket, which lifted me in the air before the truck hit me. (Disclaimer: Do not try it at home! Seriously, don't try it!)

One of our favorite pranks in the shop is to hide spiders to scare Chet Ruth, one of our mechanics. He's terrified of spiders, almost as much as I'm afraid of koala bears and clowns. I don't know what it is about them, but I don't care for them. We put fake—and live—spiders in his lunchbox, toolboxes, and anywhere else he's work-

> *He's terrified of spiders, almost as much as I'm afraid of koala bears and clowns.*

ing. When Chet sees them, he screams, hits the floor, and runs away like a little girl. We didn't know his brother Tyson was also afraid of spiders. He won't get near them, either!

One weekend, we turned Heavy D's house—the Moto Ranch—into the Redneck Olympics. We built a huge BMX ramp and jumped our bikes and motorcycles into a pond. Even better: we used the bucket of an excavator as a rope swing by tying a long bungee cord to it and flipping people into the pond. Later, we flipped people into the water while they were sitting inside a human ball. (Disclaimer again: Do not try it at home!) One of my personal favorite pranks was the time I towed a Honda Accord with the winch on my diesel truck. What can I say? I was tired of gassers parking in front of the diesel pump at gas stations!

Of course, my most legendary prank occurred, fittingly, on April Fools Day 2013. It was epic! After months of planning—okay, after a few minutes of planning—we decided to roll coal on our good friend Johnny Riche, who is vice president of production and TV talent at Rockwell Watches. Heavy D and me worked with Johnny for a couple of years, and we're still very close friends. He was an easy target to prank. We knew Johnny liked to take a two o'clock pit stop in the bathroom of his office almost every day. The day before the prank, one of our marketing guys snuck into his office and planted a camera in the bathroom.

The next day, after one of Johnny's coworkers tipped us off that he was making his way to the bathroom, we pulled our truck next to his office. We had a black irrigation pipe attached to the exhaust pipe of one of our diesel trucks. We opened a window and dropped the hose into the bathroom, while Johnny was sitting on the toilet doing his business and reading a magazine. Once we started rollin' coal into the bathroom, Johnny came running out with soot covering his face and clothes. At first he wasn't very happy about the joke. But then he realized it was a prank and had a good time with it.

We posted a video of the prank on YouTube and it quickly went viral. In fact, a few hundred thousand people watched the video in the first few days, including Jay Leno, who thought it was hilarious. He invited us to appear on *The Tonight Show* as part of his "Prank You Very Much" segment. On November 22, 2013, Johnny and I appeared onstage with Jay in Hollywood, which was a very cool experience I'll never forget. Jay liked to give a gift to the prank victims on his show, so he gave Johnny a World War II gas mask that was equipped with a roll of toilet paper. It was hilarious!

Well, shortly before April Fools Day 2014, we learned from

our inside sources at Rockwell that Johnny was planning to get even with us. At the time, we were running a contest in which we were going to give away Chevy, Dodge, and Ford trucks to three winners. Johnny was going to tow one of the trucks into the desert or put it on top of our building with a crane. Basically, he was trying to sabotage our giveaway! We knew we couldn't let it happen.

When we found out what Johnny was trying to do to us, we decided to turn the tables and literally flipped the prank on him. I drove one of our giveaway trucks to his office at Rockwell. Johnny thought I had a thing for their receptionist Rachel, who told him that she'd invited me to lunch that day. Johnny borrowed a tow truck from one of his buddies and planned to steal my truck. But Johnny didn't know that I was hiding inside the office, along with Heavy D, Red Beard, The Muscle, and some of our other guys.

After Johnny pulled up and ran around back, I unlocked the cab of his tow truck. As he started to tie the winch to my truck, we ran out of the office, firing paintballs at him. He jumped back into his cab and started to drive away. But then some of our guys ran in front of the tow truck with a big tire, forcing him to slam on the brakes. The cab flipped forward, just as we'd planned! But we didn't know Johnny wasn't wearing his seat belt, so he went crashing into the windshield, with tools, boxes, and even antifreeze crashing on top of him.

It was funny and it was great video, but it also could have gone terribly wrong. We almost watched our good friend go through the windshield of a truck because of our prank. (We still continued to hit him with paintballs, though.) When it was all said and done, Johnny had to buy the tow truck from his buddy because it was damaged. It ended up being an expensive prank for all of us.

HEAVY D: As the grown-up and mature one in this relationship, let me offer you some words of advice about pranks and practical jokes. Yes, most of the time they're harmless and good, clean fun. Hopefully our fans get a lot of enjoyment out of the crazy, wild things we do to each other. But you have to understand that our pranks are harmless, good fun because we all like each other and no one's feelings get hurt. That's what makes our pranks so funny—we have great chemistry and don't take the jokes personally.

That's what makes our pranks so funny—we have great chemistry and don't take the jokes personally.

There are a few rules you have to remember when it comes to practical jokes and pranks. Most important, make sure your practical joke doesn't go too far. We almost learned that the hard way when we unlocked the cab of Johnny's tow truck. He might have been seriously hurt or even worse. Make sure your prank won't be considered harassment; don't make fun of someone's race, gender, or religion. Don't cross that line, because it's not fun for anyone.

Second, keep your pranks reasonable. Understand the consequences of what you're about to do, and ask yourself if you'd be upset if someone else did to you what you're about to do. More times than not, the person you're pranking is probably going to try to get even, and chances are he's going to try to do something worse to you. That's the point of every prank—to try to best each other. The next prank is going to be bigger and better than the one before.

It's very important to make sure that you pick the right target. Don't choose to prank the guy at work who can't stand you or doesn't have a sense of humor. He's only going to get ticked off and won't find it funny. What's the point in pranking someone who won't laugh about it? Don't choose somebody who might have thin skin or gets upset easily. That's bullying and it's no fun for anyone. It's a lot more fun to prank your buddies and loved ones.

One of my favorite YouTube videos is the one of a guy who shoots his wife with a Nerf gun every day for a week. No matter what she's doing, he comes out of nowhere and fires a Nerf ball at her! Eventually she gets tired of it, but she doesn't take it personally because her husband is doing it. Sure, she's annoyed but it's still funny because they love each other.

Also, unless you have a close relationship with your boss, like Diesel Dave and I have, never punk a superior. It's never a good idea to question his or her authority, and it's probably also a good idea not to pull off a prank when a district manager or CEO is around. Choose the right time and place for a prank.

Don't do it when your company is facing a serious deadline. Pranks should be fun, but they shouldn't disrupt production too much.

Don't get anybody hurt, and don't tear up anything that can't be fixed.

Hey, just remember that pranks and practical jokes shouldn't be dangerous or destructive, especially at work. Don't get anybody hurt, and don't tear up anything that can't be fixed.

If you want to punk a coworker or friend, pimp out his or her ride or cover their truck with plastic wrap or aluminum foil. Maybe you can fill up the bed of the truck with packing peanuts (or horse manure). If you want to prank a coworker, cover his or her office with Post-it notes or wrap their cubicle in photocopies of a shirtless David Hasselhoff.

If you're trying to punk your loved ones or friends, give them a caramel-covered onion instead of an apple, or even a five-pound bag of Haribo sugar-free gummy bears (YouTube it, it's hilarious!). One of my favorite tricks is to seal a bar of soap with clear nail polish. Then you can watch your wife or husband scrub their bodies while trying to figure out why the bar won't lather. If your wife likes to watch TV, program the remote to where it will only turn to the Discovery Channel or ESPN. It will drive her insane as she misses *The Bachelor* or *Grey's Anatomy*.

Now, listen, this is very important: This last trick should only be used on your closest friends and loved ones. One morning, cover the toilet in your bathroom with plastic wrap and then put the seat down. Then wait for them to go No. 2. It might take them a while to forgive you for that one.

Pranks are supposed to be fun, and hopefully that's what people see when they watch our tricks on YouTube, Instagram, and Facebook. We're passionate about what we do, and we really care for each other and love one another, and that's what makes our practical jokes so much fun. It's why Johnny wasn't mad when we rolled coal on him in the bathroom.

We knew that practical joke was funny, but we had no idea how well it would be received. Within six months, more than four million people had watched the video on YouTube. It was insane. We had no idea it would lead to Diesel Dave and Johnny appearing on *The Tonight Show* with Leno. And we certainly had no idea *The Tonight Show* would only be the beginning of our TV careers.

DIESEL HANDBOOK LESSON NO. 6
SCAVENGING FOR PARTS

Let's say the used diesel truck you bought needs a little bit of work. You're going to need some parts, and it doesn't make much financial sense to go out to your local auto parts store and shell out hundreds of dollars for new components.

Not when there are several other places you can find parts—at much cheaper prices! If you're on a budget on a personal build, or you're trying to make a living flipping diesel trucks like us, you'll have spent all the money the truck's worth on new parts. You might be left dropping $2,500 on a new transmission for a 1999 Dodge Ram 1500 short cab that's worth $8,000. It doesn't make much sense! So you have to find ways to save some Benjamins by utilizing used and aftermarket parts.

Here are the best places and ways to find them:

1. Salvage yards

The good news about junkyards is that there's usually at least one in every town—and, no, I'm not talking about the local Hyundai dealership!

In most instances, the only difference between a used part and a new part is the price. For example, if you pulled a used window crank off an old Ford OBS pickup, it would probably work just as well as one you'd buy online (if you could even find one!).

We buy used parts from salvage yards all the time, and The Muscle is great at locating the parts we need. It's like sending a mouse into a maze with cheese at the end. Or, in The Muscle's case, we send him into a maze of cars and trucks and put a Whopper at the end!

Salvage yards are great places to find interior trim pieces and mechanical parts that aren't likely to wear down over time. While I wouldn't buy a transmission from a truck with more than 300,000 miles on its odometer, I'd probably buy an alternator or starter from a truck that had 50,000 miles on it.

Now, you're probably going to have to work to find the parts you need. Be patient and don't buy the first part you find, either. There might be the same part on a newer model that will also work on your truck, and it's probably going to be a better buy in the end. Also be sure to test all electronic components before you purchase them and leave the yard.

Make sure you bring your own tools to the junkyard, too. A lot of salvage yards are pick-and-pull yards, where you're required to find the part yourself—and remove it! If that's the case, you're going to need a hammer, pliers, ratchet set, hacksaw, screwdrivers, wrenches, and maybe even a pry bar. Make sure you bring sunscreen and plenty of water, too. It might be a long afternoon of scavenging.

If you're lucky, you'll find a junkyard that has employees

who are paid to find the parts for you. You only have to pick up the phone and tell them what you need. I've got a black book filled with names of guys like that across the country. It's good to get to know those guys and tip them heavily. You never know when you might need their services in the future.

2. Online search

There's a huge marketplace for used parts, none bigger than what's available online. If you look at websites like car-part.com, which boasts that it has 190 million parts, and junkpartz.com, you can search huge databases of salvage yards all over the country. You can go on those websites and enter the vehicle identification number of your truck, or search for parts by make and model. You can even choose what region of the country you want to search, or just search all fifty states.

Websites like eBay and Craigslist are also great places to search for parts. But if you buy parts from those websites, make sure it's exactly what you need, because you can't return the parts in many cases. By shopping online, you'll probably save 50 to 75 percent off what you would have paid for new parts at a retail store.

3. Insurance auctions

If the truck you're buying or rebuilding needs extensive work, you might want to consider buying a donor truck for parts. We go to salvage and insurance auctions all the time and find great deals on trucks we rebuild or use for donor parts. Sometimes you can find trucks that are discounted as much as 70 percent off the *Kelley Blue Book* value.

Heck, the Mega RamRunner was a 2012 Dodge Ram with extensive damage, and we were able to buy it for only $25,000. Now it's probably worth as much as $250,000, depending on the buyer! If we look hard enough, we might find a truck that's worth $30,000 and pay $12,000 for it! Maybe the truck was hit from behind and its back end was damaged, but we'd planned on stretching the truck and adding a flatbed anyway. The engine, interior, hood, fenders, and front end are absolutely fine and can be used in a different truck with a solid frame.

There are hundreds of insurance auctions around the country—Insurance Auto Auctions (IAAI.com) is a good place to start—and many of them advertise their inventories online and you can bid in auctions to buy them. Some of them also have buyer services programs, in which they'll connect you with a licensed broker who's experienced at auctions and will help you identify and buy what you're looking for. In most states, you have to have a license to buy vehicles from insurance auctions, so the brokers act as a middleman for you. The auction companies will also help arrange transportation to get your new truck to you.

4. Aftermarket parts

If you can't find used parts, aftermarket parts are the next-best option. There are some instances in which I think it's necessary to buy OEM (original equipment manufacturer) parts, especially when it comes to computers and other electronic components.

But in most other cases, I think you can save a considerable amount of money and find a lot more variety in aftermarket parts. Also, some of the aftermarket parts are better than the OEM parts because the kinks and defects have been eliminated. Unless you're going to a service center at a dealership, almost every repair shop and mechanic is going to use aftermarket parts about 80 percent of the time. In most cases, they're quality parts and are widely accepted. Just make sure the aftermarket parts are direct replacement parts and won't affect the truck's warranty if it's still in effect.

–Heavy D

CHAPTER ELEVEN
REALITY TV

HEAVY D: After Diesel Dave and Johnny Riche appeared on *The Tonight Show with Jay Leno* in November 2013, we probably received a dozen or so emails from TV producers wanting to talk to us about doing a reality TV show. We even had a couple of Skype conference calls with producers, who wanted to come to Salt Lake City and film us doing pranks and working in our shop to present to network or studio executives.

To be honest, we weren't all that interested in doing a TV show, and we were suspicious of the producers who were calling us. Quite frankly, we thought reality TV was probably a scam. As we mentioned earlier, Diesel Dave and I grew up in Mormon homes, and we were taught to kind of be skeptical of salesmen or people who said they could get you a deal.

In fact, we thought the TV producers who were cold-calling us were kind of like the modeling "talent scouts" who used to approach us in the shopping mall. The modeling scouts would tell us they were going to make us fashion superstars, but you don't have to look at us for very long to figure out that probably wasn't going to happen. Seriously, I mean, have you ever seen a bearded man wearing cutoff jean shorts and cowboy boots walking down a runway in Paris or New York? Diesel Dave would have a better chance of being elected governor of Utah!

Seriously, I mean have you ever seen a bearded man wearing cutoff jean shorts and cowboy boots walking down a runway in Paris or New York?

Our biggest concern about reality TV was that the producers were going to create fake story lines with artificial drama because that's what we'd seen in other shows. We're not fans of fake news! Those shows just don't seem real and a lot of other "reality" TV shows seem to be the same way. Don't get me wrong, there are quite a few entertaining reality TV shows, but too many of them seem scripted and unrealistic.

Bert Klasey, who was a senior development producer for Discovery Channel, probably called us six or seven times about meeting with him. We ignored him for several weeks, but he kept calling us back. We just weren't interested in doing a TV show. But Bert wasn't some fly-by-night producer and was persistent. He'd previously produced the A&E series *Hoarders* and the *Three Sheets* series on Spike and the Travel Channel. He was also a casting producer for ABC's *Wife Swap* and MTV's

Real World. When we finally talked to Bert in December 2013, he sounded legitimate and obviously had an impressive background.

Bert is really the person who made our show happen. He was very, very persistent but not overzealous. He was superinterested in what we were doing and thought our pranks would go over well on TV. More than anything, I think we were able to convince Bert that our day-to-day lives with the pranks, accidents, and other antics were enough drama and more interesting than us bickering among ourselves. Fighting with each other was one thing we weren't going to do. If you've seen our show, I think you can recognize that we genuinely like and love each other. It's real and there's nothing fake about it.

> *If you've seen our show, I think you can recognize that we genuinely like and love each other. It's real and there's nothing fake about it.*

Once Bert told us he was working directly with Discovery Channel—and not a production company—we trusted him and were interested in working with him. Since I'm a little bit of a science and technology nut, I've always enjoyed watching Discovery Channel. I like watching shows such as *Dirty Jobs*, *Deadliest Catch*, and *MythBusters*. I like watching documentaries and finding out how things are made and work. Plus, Discovery Channel had already enjoyed a lot of success with car-themed TV shows on their "Motor Mondays" lineup. With shows like *Fast N' Loud*, *Street Outlaws*, *American Choppers*, *Chrome Underground*, *Fat N' Furious*, *Rusted Development*, and others, Discovery Channel had a garage full of shows like ours that were popular. I thought it would be the perfect home for us.

After much discussion, we finally agreed to let Bert and his crew come to our shop in February 2014 to make a teaser video, or what they call a "sizzle reel" in Hollywood. It couldn't have been better timing—we were right in the middle of the Mega RamRunner build. Bert and his crew stayed with us for about two weeks, and then they went back to their studio to edit a sizzle reel to show to Discovery Channel.

In February 2015, we signed a contract for six episodes of *Diesel Brothers* with the Discovery Channel. Magilla Entertainment, which has produced a plethora of nonscripted TV shows like *Moonshiners* and *Rattled,* also produces our show, and Matt Ostrom, Laura Palumbo Johnson, Jason Fox, Cristin Cricco-Powell, and others have done a great job bringing us along and being patient with TV novices.

Although our series wasn't scheduled to premiere for more than a year, we had to make quite a few adjustments to our shop and businesses to prepare for the show. In January 2015, we had three mechanics and one painter at Sparks Motors and three employees working on social media and filling retail orders at DieselSellerz.

Once we moved to our new shop and prepared to start filming *Diesel Brothers* we hired three more mechanics, one more painter, and about three more employees at DieselSellerz. For us, it was a huge investment in our companies. We were looking at $50,000 to $60,000 in payroll every month, which is way more than we'd paid in the past. But it was necessary because Diesel Dave, The Muscle, Redbeard, and I would be so busy filming the show that we wouldn't have a lot of time to work on the contracted builds and other projects in our shop. As you can probably tell, the first few months of filming *Diesel Brothers* were terrifying for quite a few reasons.

DIESEL DAVE: When Heavy D approached me about doing a reality TV show, I really didn't know what to think. Since I'd spent much of the previous four or five years living at our shop or in an RV out back, I didn't watch a lot of TV, and I certainly didn't know what reality TV was about. In fact, the only reality TV I'd ever watched was when I talked to myself in the mirror (which, believe it or not, happens a lot when you're living in an RV alone). But I knew one thing: reality TV might be an opportunity for us to expand our business in a big way, which is something we desperately needed to do.

About the time Bert contacted us about doing a TV show, we were in pretty rough shape financially. We'd made a pretty big mistake and were still trying to climb our way out of a sizable hole. We'd just finished our second truck giveaway—Jason Ruark of Salisbury, Maryland, won our rebuilt 2013 Ford F-250 Super Duty on January 1, 2014—and it produced about $500,000 in retail sales for us. That might sound like a good thing, but there was one big problem.

An order had mistakenly gone in for $60,000 worth of the same shirt. Making matters worse, shortly after the order was made in December 2013, we received a cease-and-desist order from a company who owned the trademark on the T-shirt slogan we'd ordered. As a result, we couldn't sell the T-shirts, and there are probably about 15,000 kids in Mozambique who are wearing them now. We also had to refund money to the people who'd ordered them, and we didn't have any other T-shirt designs. Obviously, that mistake almost buried us.

On top of that dilemma, our traffic on Facebook and other social media sites had kind of started to plateau. Facebook put controls on its advertising that made it more difficult for companies like DieselSellerz to reach consumers, and our videos and truck ads weren't generating the same kind of traffic they once were. We needed a new way to get exposure, and thankfully the TV show came to fruition around the same time.

Now, the original plan for the TV show was to film six episodes in six months to keep production costs down. In those six months, the producers wanted us to build nine vehicles. I don't care how talented our mechanics and engineers are—that's unrealistic. Nobody can work that fast. Then Discovery Channel placed an order for two more episodes and it wanted them in ten months. After only a few months, we were so far behind schedule that the producers had to push back the date of our debut episode.

On January 4, 2016, *Diesel Brothers* finally made its debut, and, to be honest, the odds were stacked against us. We were slotted right behind *Fast N' Loud*, which is a show about the Gas Monkey Garage in Dallas, which buys, restores, and re-sells forgotten, derelict cars. Basically, they do what we do, but with classic American cars from a 1931 Ford Model A to a 1973 Pontiac Trans Am. Those guys are great mechanics and personalities, and they were much more established among TV viewers than us. They had a huge following, and we weren't sure their fans would stick around to watch us.

Thankfully, most of the fans who followed us on Facebook and Instagram tuned in to watch the first episode of *Diesel Brothers*. In the premiere, we transformed a rusty 1948 Willys Jeep into a diesel-drinking monster and found our next give-away truck at a gas station, where we bought a pristine 2007 Chevy 2500 with an LBZ Duramax diesel engine for $5,500. It was identical to the first truck Heavy D ever owned, and he had to have it. Our debut episode ranked in the top ten in ratings for original cable telecasts that night—way ahead of shows like *Conan*, *The Daily Show*, and *Hannity*—and it was Discovery Channel's highest-rated premiere in four years. We all let out a huge sigh of relief after that first episode because we didn't know what to expect.

In our first season, we averaged more than two million viewers per episode, which was Discovery Channel's highest-rated new series among adults aged 25 to 54 in two years. We can't thank our fans enough for watching, and we attribute a lot of the success from our first season to social media. After only four episodes, Discovery Channel announced that it was extending its order for sixteen more episodes. Oddly enough, after our first eight episodes, some of our fans thought our series had been canceled, because it was several months before new episodes aired. That's how long it takes to make TV, folks!

CHAPTER TWELVE
THE CREW

HEAVY D: To be honest, I never know when I might come up with a concept for a crazy, cool truck.

It might happen when I'm sleeping, taking a shower, eating, or sitting in church on Sunday morning. Now, if you know anything

> To be honest, I never know when I might come up with a concept for a crazy, cool truck.

about business, you know that coming up with a truly great idea is only half the battle. The other half is executing the plan and that's the part that requires a lot of blood, sweat, and tears. That's why it's so critical to have the right people in place to help you carry out the plan and execute your vision.

If you've watched *Diesel Brothers*, you're probably familiar with Diesel Dave, Redbeard, The Muscle, and me. But you might not know a lot about the most important people in our operation—the ones who work behind the scenes to help us build our trucks and get them running exactly right, publicize them on social media, and make sure our companies are finely tuned operations. Without our mechanics, auto body repairers, painters, marketing and social media experts, retail managers, warehouse workers, and others, Diesel Power Gear, Sparks Motors, and DieselSellerz.com would have never become nationally recognized brands.

The guys in our shop are the heart and soul of our operation. I might be the guy who comes up with the blueprints for our trucks, but our mechanics and technicians are the guys who pour the concrete, lay the bricks, and do the framing. They're much more knowledgeable about engines, transmissions, and suspensions than Diesel Dave and me, and they're absolutely artists with sockets, wrenches, and ratchets in their hands.

They're absolutely artists with sockets, wrenches, and ratchets in their hands.

Two of our mechanics, Chris and Jose, who are brothers from Mexico, have been with us since the very beginning. They were with us when we worked out of a small shop on the Rockwell yard. They're very loyal guys and extremely hard workers. Whether it's construction, landscaping, or automotive, they have the mentality that even if they don't know how to do something, they're going to figure it out. When there isn't a build to do, we'll send them up to my house to do work just to keep them busy. They're religious guys and their faith is important to them, which is probably why there's nothing but positive words coming out of their mouths. They're constantly giving people high fives or a thumbs-up, and they really establish the foundation for the positive atmosphere in our shop.

More than anything, Chris and Jose love to work and they never complain. Even after we expanded our staff in the shop, they're still the fastest ones at getting things done. We haven't found anyone who can match their combination of speed, work ethic, and talents. Other guys might be as skilled or knowledgeable, but they're not nearly as fast or dedicated. Chris and Jose have been with us the longest, and they're as valuable as anyone we have.

Steve Carroll is our lead mechanic and head honcho in the shop. Steve was a guy I had communicated with quite a bit on off-road and diesel forums on the Internet. I knew Steve only by his handle on message boards and didn't know him personally. But whenever we had a problem or an issue in the shop, Steve was the guy who always seemed to have a solution. He grew up in Harrisburg, Oregon, and actually worked on diesel trains before he came on board with us. He helped us build the Mega RamRunner for the SEMA show in Las Vegas, and then we brought him on full-time and made him our shop foreman in October 2014.

While Steve was working on the railroad, he had a passion for building and driving diesel trucks. His personal vehicle was a 1999 Chevrolet OBS truck with a short bed, and he also owned a Chevy Camaro. But his prized possession might have been a 2002 Chevy Trailblazer that he converted into a mud truck and rock climber. As you can tell, Steve is a Chevy guy. Of course, Steve also had to have a 2004 Freightliner with a 16-foot flatbed to haul his vehicles around. Steve is great at finding run-down classic trucks in barns and other places around the country.

What I appreciate about Steve the most is that he tells it like it is and doesn't sugarcoat things.

What I appreciate about Steve the most is that he tells it like it is and doesn't sugarcoat things.

When we start a project, he's going to tell me absolutely everything that's wrong with a truck we're going to rebuild. Whether it's a flat tire, broken bolt, rusty floor, busted transmission, or bad axles, Steve is going to identify the problems and figure out a way to fix them. He'll show us every flaw that needs to be corrected to make the truck perfect. His creativity comes from devising ways to fix problems.

Chet Ruth is a welder and fabricator in our shop, and we hired him after we met him while racing dirt bikes in the desert. Chet grew up on a ranch in Mesquite, Nevada, and he worked in the oil fields before he came to us. Even better: he recruited his older brother Tyson to come work for us, too. They're sunup-to-sundown kind of guys and don't quit until the job is done. They know how to get things done and are very dedicated to their crafts. The thing I love about them the most is they'll roll up their sleeves, go to work, and never complain. Aside from a few sibling squabbles in the shop, Chet and Tyson are best friends and work great together.

Chavis Fryer is our in-house Duramax expert and performance specialist. The guy has some serious body ink, abs, and Duramax knowledge. He came on board about the same time as Steve and is well known in the diesel world as a top engine mechanic. I swear the guy could get a cat that used each of its nine lives purring again. He understands the heart and soul of a truck and what makes it tick. Chavis built and raced the Reaper, our performance truck, and he's also competed in the National Hot Rod Diesel Association Big Sky Truck Fest.

Ryan Morgan, one of our fabricators and engineers, can do absolutely anything with metal. That's why we call him "Mor-Gyver." Give the guy a sheet of metal, a welding torch, and a mallet, and he could probably build you a submarine—or at least a rocket. He's that good. Pace "PZ" Michael is another welder and fabricator in our shop and does fantastic work of his own, and Primo and Martin run our paint booth. Regardless of what Diesel Dave might say, there are more available colors at Sparks Motors than just gray. D. J. Purser takes care of everything in the interior of a truck—electrical, lighting, and instruments. He's in charge of making sure all the instruments work and look good.

Hans Peterson, from Blackfoot, Idaho, is probably the youngest guy and smallest guy in the shop, but he's in charge of all of the roughneck mechanics and does a good job of keeping order. I think the other guys respect Hans because he's not afraid to jump in and offer a helping hand on builds. Once they realized Hans knew what he was doing, they figured out he was one of us.

Once we started building trucks for the TV show, we convinced the guys from Overkill Racing and Chassis from Masilla, New Mexico, to basically move into our shop. As their company name suggests, they overkill everything, which is fantastic. Joel Buschmann, who started the company, grew up in Littleton, Colorado, and played football at New Mexico State University.

When his playing career ended, Joel was in the cellular molecular biology PhD program at New Mexico State and built monster trucks out of his two-car garage as a hobby. But when Joel's truck named Overkill finished in the top fifty out of 58,000 entrants at the 2012 SEMA show, he dropped out of the doctorate program and started building trucks full-time. Now Joel and his guys design trucks on computers and build rock buggies, ultra 4x4s, monster trucks, and mega mud trucks. They do unbelievably awesome work and it's great that they're working with us side by side.

DIESEL DAVE: Sure, we might build awesome trucks that look great and are a blast to drive, but if the folks in our marketing and retail departments didn't help run our contests and sell merchandise and apparel, we wouldn't have the money to build them. Just ask Redbeard! Obviously for those reasons, our marketing, social media, and retail employees are as valuable and integral to our companies as our mechanics and paint and body guys.

Like Chris and Jose, Jackknife Jim Anderson has worked with us since the very beginning. I told you about Jim earlier; we traveled across South America on motorbikes together before we came back to Utah to work for Heavy D. Jim is one of our best friends, and we call him the "Captain of Adventure" around the shop. He's always looking for something fun and extreme to do, whether it's jumping out of a helicopter into a lake, motorcycling up the Pacific Coast Highway, or snowplowing a driveway to Heavy D's cabin. He's the general manager of Sparks Motors, and if someone comes to our place looking to buy a truck, they'll talk and negotiate with Jim. He's great at following up with potential buyers, which is something Heavy D and I are not very good at doing.

Frankly, we're lucky Jim is still here with us. In October 2016, a 12,000-pound truck accidentally popped into reverse and rolled over his legs. The truck nearly crushed him. We feared Jim broke both of his legs and shattered his pelvis, which might have left him paralyzed. If the truck had rolled another three or four inches over him, it might have killed him. It was a very scary time for all of us. Fortunately, he was left with two fractures on the right side of his pelvis, along with some very bad bruising. After several grueling weeks of rehab, Jim came back to work with us. Jim has no doubt his life was spared, and that the good Lord had other plans for him. Most important, he is still here to help his wife, Macie, raise their beautiful daughter, Iyla.

John Whiting, whom you might know as "Brown Dog Millionaire" from *Diesel Brothers*, grew up with Redbeard in Roosevelt, Utah, and they're best friends. We hired Brown Dog as our warehouse manager in 2014 and then promoted him to general manager of Diesel Power Gear, our main retail website. Brown Dog Millionaire is kind of like the Evil Monkey or Ernie the Giant Chicken in *Family Guy*; he has a recurring role on *Diesel Brothers* and you never quite know when he's going to show up. But when he does, it takes you a while to forget what you saw! You might see him getting blown out of a chair in one show, then not see him for a couple of episodes. If your order gets lost in the mail, Brown Dog Millionaire is the guy you call. When you reach him, he'll probably be climbing rocks, mountain biking, watching the Utah Jazz, or trying to perfect the world's greatest beef jerky. He's also the reigning Diesel Power Gear fantasy football champion. Just ask him. There are a lot of great people, including my sister Amber and Heavy D's mom Lisa, working in our warehouse filling retail orders under Brown Dog Millionaire's supervision.

Braden Simar is a talented graphic designer we hired in November 2014. He was working at a UPS Store when we discovered some of his work online. Now he designs most of our T-shirts, hats, and other apparel, as well as our websites and artwork for our social media posts. He is a very talented artist and our fans love his work. Kollin Brinkerhoff shoots the videos you see on our Web pages and social media channels, along with Van Oakes, Josh "Burnout" Thompson, and Ryan Scott. Kyle Wells is our company photographer, and he's tasked with making us look pretty. Good luck with that!

While Braden comes up with the designs for our stuff, Didi Joy calls herself the "Internet overlord" of our operations. She has a bachelor of science degree in psychology from the University of Utah, which certainly comes in handy when you're working with a bunch of grease monkeys, and she's very smart when it comes to computers and the Internet. Basically, whenever one of our websites isn't working, Didi is the person who gets it up and running again. Plus, Didi has really cool hair. She's kind of like Katy Perry; you never know what color it's going to be on a given day.

Plus, Didi has really cool hair. She's kind of like Katy Perry; you never know what color it's going to be on a given day.

Paige Camryn is another pretty face that greets our customers and handles inside retail sales. We knew Paige in high school, and then she got married and moved to the East Coast. She came back to Utah in 2013, and we hired her to work in marketing and social media. She answers emails and takes care of customers in the retail space at the front of our building. Paige has two beautiful kids, and she'll kick your butt on the golf course and ski slopes.

The people who work in our shop, warehouse, and social

media and marketing departments are more than employees. They're our close friends and some of them are literally our family. All of them have played critical roles in helping our companies grow and expand in a very short time, and we couldn't have done it without each of them.

DIESEL HANDBOOK LESSON NO. 7
TRICKING OUT A TRUCK

Let's say you've just purchased your first diesel truck. It's a good one—a 2003 Dodge Ram 2500 with a Cummins 5.9-liter engine. Now, if you didn't have to break the bank to buy your first diesel, hopefully there's some money left in your pocket to customize your truck.

Hey, if you're like me, you definitely don't want to be driving a truck that looks like the one your grandpa drives down the gravel road to get his mail every afternoon.

Luckily, there are quite a few accessories that are pretty cost-efficient to customize your truck. Here are ten examples of what you can do:

1. Install an air horn.

Remember that your truck horn is going to be a lot like the "like" button on Facebook—it's going to be one of the most important things you use and you're going to use it a lot! If somebody cuts you off on the highway or you need to tell an antelope to get out of the way, you don't want your truck sounding like a shrieking fifth-grade girl. You want it to sound like something ferocious. That's why my horn sounds like an AK-47. People get out of the way when I use it! You can purchase a 15-inch air horn with a mini direct drive compressor for about $125 on dieselpowergear.com. It's worth it.

2. Change the headlights.

If the truck you purchased is nearly fifteen years old, chances are the headlight covers are dirty or fogged over, and the headlights probably aren't bright enough to see ten feet in front of you. Plus, today's headlights aren't yesterday's headlights. They look pretty sweet. You can get a pair of Spyder projector LED halo headlights and matching LED taillights for about $475. Hey, you have to be able to see where you're going!

3. Add an exhaust tip.

An exhaust tip isn't going to change anything about the way your truck runs, but it is going to make it sound a lot deeper. It's like going from Adam Levine to Johnny Cash. And it's going to look a lot better than the stock tailpipe, which is probably filthy and rusted by now. An exhaust tip is like the cherry on an ice cream sundae. It's really just bling. You can purchase an AFE Logo six-inch black tip that looks really good for about $150.

4. Tint the windows.

Tinting your truck's windows is very cost-effective, and it's going to keep the inside of the cab comfortable and cool during the summer. Plus, it's going to prevent nosy drivers from seeing what you're doing at stoplights! Remember what I said about chicks digging trucks? Tint your windows, brother!

The average cost of window tinting is anywhere from $150 to $400, depending on the quality of the material and whether or not there's a sliding window in the rear of the cab. Be sure to check state laws about tinting. A few states have banned it without medical prescriptions and other states limit how dark the tint can be.

5. Install a leveling or lift kit.

Depending on how high you want to lift your truck and how much money you want to spend, there are several options to get your truck higher. A body lift uses spring spacers with blocks made of rubber or polyurethane and works well if you don't want to alter the stock suspension. Leveling kits balance the height of your truck from front to back and create about a two-inch lift, and they're relatively cheap at around $130. If you're willing to spend a little more money, a premium lift kit such as the Pro Comp six-inch lift kit costs about $1,625 and will transform your truck into a badass monster.

6. Add new wheels and tires.

You'll be surprised by how much new wheels and tires will change the look of your truck. It's kind of like when your momma gives you new church shoes! Wheels can cost any-where from $200 apiece to much, much more. And depending on the size of the wheels, the cost of new Patriot tires is going to vary as well. If you have a six-inch lift, you're probably going to want 20-inch wheels and 37-inch Patriot tires or it's not going to look right. If you have a two-inch lift, you can get away with smaller wheels and tires.

7. Replace the differential covers.

If you're driving a 4x4 truck—and I'm not sure why you'd be driving anything else—you probably should consider replacing your stock differential covers. There's one on both the front and rear axles and they're built to protect the hardware and gears that make the wheels spin. The differential covers also house oil and help keep it clean and cool.

Stock differential covers usually aren't very thick or durable, which can be a problem when you're riding trails or climbing rocks. If one is cracked or busted open, you're going to lose oil and potentially damage expensive internal components. Or you're going to be stranded in the middle of nowhere until help arrives! I'd suggest replacing the front and rear covers, and you can buy a pair of AFE heavy-duty aluminum covers for about $520. They're well worth the investment.

8. Install leather seats.

If you purchased a truck with leather seats, the rawhide is probably worn and faded by now, and the same goes for cloth seats, which are probably filthy. You wouldn't believe how easy it is now to replace the upholstery in your truck with custom leather seats.

Our friends at leatherseats.com have factory-style leather seat covers, with full leather facing and vinyl on the sides and backs of the front seats and a combination of leather and vinyl in the bench, for less than $1,000. They're double-stitched, plush, and very durable. The front seat covers even come with the Ram logo! For a little more money, you can even customize the leather to the exact way you want it.

9. Replace the grille.

Hey, when you reach a certain age (or if you didn't brush your teeth like how your parents told you), you're probably going to need some serious dental work done. Maybe you grind your teeth, eat too much candy, or don't floss like you're supposed to. Regardless of why, you might need a new grille. Everybody wants to have nice, shiny teeth because your smile is the first thing people notice.

Trucks aren't any different. The grille is going to be the first thing people see coming down the street, and it might as well look good. You can replace the stock grille with an RX Series studded chrome grille for about $945. Then you might want a grille guard to protect it. Nobody wants bugs (or deer) in their teeth.

10. Get a bedliner.

If you're using your truck like it's supposed to be used, you're probably hauling concrete bags, lumber, tools, and other stuff around. Before you scratch up the bed too much, get a bedliner to protect it from dents and dings (and eventual rust).

There are more than a few options. There's a do-it-yourself application that costs about $125. Then there are one-piece, drop-in bedliners that cost about $250. The best protection is a spray-in bedliner and it's going to cost you anywhere from $350 to $500. Of course, if you really want to protect your truck from the hazards of rocks and other debris, spray the entire body in bedliner. Then it will look really sweet!

—Diesel Dave

CHAPTER THIRTEEN
MEGA RAMRUNNER

HEAVY D: You know what they say about one man's junk—it can be another man's treasure. Perhaps no one knows that better than us. We found the truck that would become the mascot of our company at an auto insurance auction in the summer of 2013. If you didn't know, insurance auctions are a great place to find cars and trucks to rebuild. It's where you can purchase salvageable vehicles at discounted prices, sometimes at 70 percent below *Kelley Blue Book* values. Now, that's a steal!

The 2012 Dodge Ram 3500 truck we bought at auction for $25,000 had been wrecked and rolled over. Its roof had collapsed, its windows were smashed, and its doors and fenders were ruined. In other words, it was perfect for what we wanted to do to it. We had big plans for the truck. We wanted to build a badass Baja truck that had the power, chassis, and suspension needed to handle desert trails and jumps. But our truck wouldn't be like any other Baja racer.

We'd started working with Mega X 2, a company in Kanosh, Utah, that had been stretching trucks for the logging industry for more than three decades. We decided to stretch the Dodge Ram 3500 into a six-door truck that still had the power and suspension needed to run in the desert—and just about anywhere else. We shipped the bone-stock Dodge to Mega X 2, which used three doors to stretch our truck. Two doors came from a Dodge Mega Cab and a window came from the door of a Dodge Durango. They flipped the window upside down and pieced the doors together. That was the most challenging part of the stretching process.

Once the stretching was complete, we built the suspension for the truck and customized the lift. By the time we were finished, there wasn't much left of the original truck, outside of the frame and the part of the chassis that hadn't been stretched. We stuffed a 600-horsepower Cummins diesel engine under the hood. The Cummins fed power to a Ford 4R100 four-speed transmission, which came from the guys at Diesel Conversion Specialists. Then we installed a pair of Axle Tech 4000 planetary axles, which are rated at a whopping nine tons and weigh 1,500 pounds each. The heavy-duty axles were designed for mine-resistant military vehicles and aren't usually available to the public. The axles were held in place by a fully custom four-link suspension up front with dual F-O-A coil-overs that are used in desert racing. The rear axle was leaf sprung with a pair of F-O-A shocks for a smooth ride, regardless of the terrain.

Of course, it wouldn't have been a Sparks Motors rebuild without plenty of upgrades. We installed four LED cubes in the front Fusion bumper, along with two in the RaceMesh Trucks grille. We installed four more LED cubes in the custom ECO tint headlights, and a Diesel Power Gear 50-inch curved bar sat right above the windshield. Believe me, there was enough wattage on that truck to light up the Grand Canyon on an overcast night. On the back of the truck, there were two Monster swivel hooks and six more LED cubes so I could see when I had to pull Diesel Dave's truck out of a ditch. Without a doubt, my favorite feature on the truck was two custom-made quad Octostackz exhaust pipes that sounded like a baritone.

When we were finished with our renovation, the crumbled-up, rolled-over Dodge Ram 3500 we purchased at auction was a rebuilt classic. We called it the Mega RamRunner and it made its debut at the 2014 SEMA trade show in Las Vegas. The SEMA (Specialty Equipment Market Association) show is the premier convention for automotive specialty products in the world. More than 60,000 domestic and international buyers flock to the SEMA show every year, and the Mega RamRunner was the most celebrated build at the 2014 show. It was our coming-out party.

The Mega RamRunner was different from any other truck out there. It weighed 14,200 pounds, which is double the weight of a standard Dodge Ram 3500. It had three sunroofs and spacious seating for eight. Its frame was stretched to an overall length about five feet longer than a standard long bed, leaving it with a 218-inch wheelbase. It barely even fit in the Fusion Bumper stall at the SEMA show. The top of the truck's cab sat about 100 inches off the ground and the back bumper was about 42 inches high because of a 16-inch lift. It had 43-inch Goodyear military tires. You almost needed a ladder to climb in the cab.

The Mega RamRunner might have started as a heap of junk, but we transformed it into an iconic masterpiece. The combination of power, beauty, precision, and downright manliness was uniquely magnificent. It was like Leonardo da Vinci's *Mona Lisa*, F. Scott Fitzgerald's *The Great Gatsby*, and Beethoven's *Symphony No. 5*.

> *It was like Leonardo da Vinci's Mona Lisa, F. Scott Fitzgerald's The Great Gatsby, and Beethoven's Symphony No. 5.*

Okay, maybe I'm getting a little carried away. Still, it was a badass truck that you could drive anywhere, whether it was in the desert, mountains, snow, or highway (at least in Utah, where it was street legal).

The coolest thing about the Mega RamRunner was that once it debuted at SEMA, its legend only seemed to grow. We posted videos on social media showcasing its unique capabilities, and it quickly became one of the most popular trucks in the world. People across the country wanted to see how far we could push the truck. We took the Mega RamRunner to the Sand Flats Recreation Area near Moab, Utah, during the Easter Jeep Safari. It conquered Hell's Gate, a white-knuckled, stomach-churning trail, and then it ascended Potato Salad Hill, which really isn't a trail, but a steep, slick rock that has left many vehicles rolling and tumbling into the ravine below. It crushed nearly every trail at Moab and barely broke a sweat.

Mountains and wicked trails weren't Mega RamRunner's only victims. It had a tug-of-war with a 1992 Marmon semitruck and held its own, even though the semi had eighteen gears and was capable of pulling 150,000 pounds. Another time, Mega Ram-Runner destroyed two trucks—one with a Cummins engine and another with a Ford Power Stroke—that were pulling against it at the same time! I even raced the Mega Ram-Runner and pulled a sled at the National Hot Rod Diesel Association Texas Diesel Nationals in Ennis, Texas.

Mountains and wicked trails weren't Mega RamRunner's only victims.

I think people were genuinely surprised to see what we were willing to do with a truck that was probably worth more than $100,000. That's one thing about us: we're not afraid to push our trucks to the limit and get them dirty. Even though our trucks might look nice and cost a boatload of money to build, we don't design them to only be parked or driven on highways. We build trucks that look good with a lot of bells and whistles, but we also want them to run well and be functional.

I have to be honest: over time, the Mega RamRunner became more like my baby and personal truck. People drove to our headquarters from all over the country to see the truck in person. Wherever I went, people recognized the truck, and I was constantly posing for photographs with it. It was almost as if we were inseparable. Our company became singularly identified with the Mega RamRunner.

That's why Diesel Dave and the rest of our crew were stunned when I decided in October 2016 to give the truck away in one of our contests. In fact, Diesel Dave and the guys wanted to have me drug tested. It was like Anheuser-Busch giving away the Clydesdales, Progressive Insurance firing Flo, or Geico replacing its gecko with a Chihuahua. The Mega RamRunner was our mascot and most prized accomplishment. My crew wasn't the only people who couldn't believe we were giving it away. Once we made the announcement on social media, our fans didn't think we were serious. In fact, they believed it was a publicity stunt or hoax. But when I confirmed the contest at the 2016 SEMA show in Las Vegas, I think people figured out that we were dead serious.

Even though the Mega RamRunner had a special place in my heart, I figured it was time for someone else to have it. I'd never held on to a truck for two years, and I was ready for a new build. Plus, by giving away our most iconic truck ever, it was going to be the greatest giveaway in our company's history.

DIESEL DAVE: I couldn't believe that Heavy D wanted to part ways with the Mega RamRunner. It was like Bo and Luke Duke selling the General Lee, Starsky and Hutch giving away their Gran Torino, or Magnum P.I. putting his Ferrari 308 GTS on Craigslist. When Heavy D told me what he planned to do, I shook my head and asked, "Are you serious, dude?" Like Heavy D said earlier, when he gets tired of something, he quits it. As hard as it is to imagine, he was tired of driving the Mega RamRunner and wanted to move on to the next big thing.

Of course, we couldn't just give away the Mega Ram-Runner. We'd put it through a lot of abuse in the previous two years, and it was due for some serious TLC from the Diesel Brothers crew. It had been through hell and back. Once Heavy D made up his mind for good, the Mega RamRunner was sent to the Sparks Motors shop for a much-needed "refresh." And by refresh, I mean that the truck was stripped to the chassis and rebuilt completely from the ground up.

Our guys removed all the old decals, and the body was sanded, primed, repainted, cut, and buffed. The underside of the body was treated with a nice thick layer of bedliner, which protects the cab from rocks and mud and also provides an adequate noise buffer. The frame of the truck was also media blasted, which involves using pressurized air to shoot tiny pieces of media (usually walnut shells, plastic beads, or aluminum oxide) to remove paint and rust and smooth scratches, dents, and gouges on metal. By the time we were done material blasting the truck, it was as smooth as a baby's bottom. Then we strengthened and coated the frame with a thick layer of rust-preventing paint.

One thing that we do with all of our giveaways is offer a cash prize instead of the truck. The winner of the Mega Ram-Runner, Chris from California, showed up and instantly fell in love with the truck. But then he was faced with the very difficult decision of choosing between the truck or the cash. At the end the day, Chris ended up taking the cash prize, because the Mega RamRunner was a little too big for him—he couldn't fit it in his garage at home in California. That was a bittersweet day for Heavy D. He'd already said goodbye to his truck, but then ended up not having to give it away. Ultimately, it's a fairy tale with a happy ending.

CHAPTER FOURTEEN
THE BUILDS

HEAVY D: One of my favorite movies as a kid was *Indiana Jones and the Last Crusade*, in which Indiana Jones and his father searched for the Holy Grail. According to legend, the grail is the cup that Jesus Christ drank from during the Last Supper, and which was used to capture his blood when he was crucified. The grail is supposed to have supernatural powers that provide happiness and eternal youth to whoever possesses it. You know, it's kind of like that feeling you get when you own a diesel truck.

Of course, *Holy Grail* also refers to those items that are the rarest of rare and most desirable in pop culture. When you hear somebody refer to the Holy Grail, they might be talking about, for instance, a T206 Honus Wagner baseball card from the early twentieth century, one of which was auctioned for $2.1 million in 2007. Or maybe it's an Action Comics No. 1 issue from 1938, which is worth $3.2 million, or an Inverted Jenny postage stamp—the one with the upside-down airplane—that's worth an estimated $997,000. Hey, find one of those items in your attic or inside a coffee can in your backyard and you're having a really good day.

When it comes to diesel trucks, the Holy Grail is a Dodge Ram built from 1996 to 1998, which was when they were equipped with a 12-valve, 5.9-liter Cummins engine and a six-speed manual transmission. With those two components, a Dodge Ram built in that time frame is considered the holiest of holy. Those were the last years Dodge put a 12-valve engine in its trucks; it replaced them with a more modernized 24-valve engine in mid-1998. But a 12-valve engine, which is easy to recognize because of its individual valve covers, is considered among diesel enthusiasts one of the longest-lasting engines out there. Think about it: there aren't any computers to make it break. Some people have put 400,000 miles on those 12-valve engines! And, with more than 400 pounds of torque and 200 horsepower, it is pretty doggone powerful, too.

That's why a 1996 Dodge Ram 2500 SLT we gave away in the MTN OPS Truck for a Buck contest in November 2015 is one of my all-time favorite builds. When we acquired the Dodge Ram, it was an old farm truck. It had a four-door crew cab and long bed. It was a very solid truck, but we still gave it our typical TLC. We added a Fusion front bumper, custom hood, Mallory Engineering custom headache rack, and

38-inch Toyo tires on American Force wheels. With a custom two-tone paint job and a completely black leather interior, it was a bad-looking truck. Believe me: you wouldn't have needed a limo for the prom if you'd owned this truck in high school.

What we installed under the hood was even better, though. We added Industrial Injection compound twin turbos with RS120 injectors, and a Dragonfly P-pump to the 12-valve engine. We also swapped out the transmission for a Dodge NV5600 six-speed. When we were finished with that truck, it

When we were finished with that truck, it was the dream of all dreams. It was the truck of trucks. It was the Holy Grail.

was the dream of all dreams. It was the truck of trucks. It was the Holy Grail.

Skyler Carter of Colby, Kansas, ended up winning the Holy Grail from us. He was deer hunting with his girlfriend in Nebraska when he found out he'd won. As he was sitting in a deer stand, his phone was blowing up with text messages, emails, and phone calls from his family and friends. He finally answered when his best friend called. When his buddy told him he'd won the Holy Grail, Skyler told him he'd better not be lying or he'd kick him you-know-where! Now, that's friendship.

Another of my favorite builds is a truck we called Hercules. It was a 2008 Chevrolet Crew Cab LT with a Duramax diesel engine. It came to us on a flatbed trailer after its face was smashed in during a head-on collision. Obviously, it needed a lot of work. We decided to transform the Duramax into a purpose-built mud truck that could handle just about anything. Our buddies at Overkill Racing and Chassis built a subframe with almost 250 feet of two-inch pipe and sat it on two massive Axle Tech 4000 axles. They put F-O-A coil-over shocks and bypass shocks on all four corners to make the ride even smoother.

Under the hood, we added Fleece Cheetah turbo, ARP head studs, Mass-Flo injectors, and an S&B cold air intake system. When we were finished, the truck stood 11 feet tall and was 20 feet long. It was so badass. We painted it gray, but hopefully its new owner will have it covered in mud. If you can no longer tell what color your truck is, that's when you know you're doing it right. That's how much we love the environment—we cover our trucks in it! We've used Hercules for just about everything, from pulling a sled at the Weekend on the Edge at Golden Spikes Arena in Ogden, Utah, to smashing a Prius in our parking lot. Hercules is one of the biggest and baddest trucks we've ever built. There isn't another truck like it.

Another truck I'll never forget is the Workhorse, which we gave away with a custom 40-foot trailer. We gave the 2013 Dodge Ram 5500 Tradesman SLT away in our Working Class giveaway in October 2016. With a 6.7-liter Cummins engine and Aisin auto transmission, the Tradesman is a reliable and powerful truck to start with, but the truck we had was white, bone stock, and pretty vanilla. We did away with the dual tires in the rear. Then we updated the transmission and T-case, which allowed it to pull a whopping 29,600 pounds of weight. We also installed an S&B cold air intake system to help the engine breathe.

We gave the Workhorse a new coat of metallic black paint and a Bradford Built flatbed that is nearly 12 feet long and 8 feet wide. On top of that, we threw in a LoadMax Low Pro Gooseneck Trailer with a custom 40-foot steel deck. Altogether, we produced the ultimate truck for the working class. Rod Elliott of Idaho Falls, Idaho, was the lucky winner.

DIESEL DAVE: As we told you earlier, both of our dads served in the military, so we've always had a ton of respect and a soft spot in our hearts for the men and women who serve in the U.S. armed forces.

> *We've always had a ton of respect and a soft spot in our hearts for the men and women who serve in the U.S. armed forces.*

They're real American heroes, and we wouldn't get to do what we do without the sacrifices they make to preserve our freedom. That's why we try to honor the military in at least one of our builds every year.

One of my favorite builds was the U.S. Duramax, which we gave away in the Self-D & DieselSellerz Truck for a

Buck contest in May 2015. We took a 2004 Chevy Silverado 2500 HD with a single cab and added a custom military trailer to it. The bed came from a 1960s M101 Cargo trailer, and we cut, stretched it, and turned it into a short bed for the truck. There was a 6.6-liter Duramax engine under the hood, and we added Fleece Performance Cheetah turbo and injectors and an injection pump from Dynomite Diesel Products to produce about 700 horsepower. Our buddies at No Zone Diesel dropped an automatic Allison transmission in it, and that baby would move!

We gave the U.S. Duramax a 12-inch lift with Sparks Motors custom suspension—long arm in the front and leaf sprung in the rear—and finished it off with 20-inch Anthem Off-Road wheels and 46-inch Goodyear tires. With a Fusion front bumper, custom grille and hood, Fiberwerx fender flares, Monster hooks, and sweet bedliner paint, it was a military-style vehicle that was ready to go to work—in the mud!

Zach Spicer of Denver, Colorado, won the U.S. Duramax, but we made him work for it a little bit. We invited him to mid-July Madness, a mud bog, redneck sled pull, and pull-off we host in West Valley, Utah. We made him think he was one of ten finalists for the U.S. Duramax, but that really wasn't the case. After Zach rode in the truck through the mud, we told him the truck was his to keep. It was a one-of-a-kind truck that took a long time to design and build.

Another truck that I'll never forget is the oMega, which we

gave away in February 2016. It was a 2013 Dodge Ram Mega Cab 3500 SLT, which is one of the newest trucks we've given away. It had a 6.7-liter Cummins engine with an automatic transmission. It was a four-door crew cab with a short bed, and it was really in good shape when we got our hands on it. Of course, we gave the oMega an eight-inch lift and put matte black Method Race Fat Five 20-inch wheels on it with 37-inch Patriot tires. Other than adding an S&B cold air intake system and having our buddies at PPEI custom-tune the engine, we didn't have to do a lot of work under the hood. It was already a bad ride. We painted it white, which looked really good with the black wheels and custom grille.

Brian Weaver of Granger, Indiana, ended up winning the oMega. We had to call him a couple of times because he wouldn't answer the phone; he thought it was somebody calling from a U.S. presidential campaign! Eventually, he flew to Salt Lake City to pick up his new truck and drove it home.

Two other very cool trucks we gave away were the Denali and White Magic, which was a 2015 Chevy Silverado 3500 LTZ with a 6.6-liter LML Duramax engine and automatic Allison transmission. Like the oMega, White Magic was in really good shape because it was so new. We added a 6½-inch lift, 37-inch Patriot tires, matte black Anthem 20-inch wheels, and a custom black bedliner. Shane Miller of Tuscarora, Pennsylvania, won White Magic. He was driving home from work when his phone started blowing up. He checked our website and saw that the winner was from Pennsylvania, and then he saw his name. He was floored.

If you didn't know, Denali comes from the Native American word for "great one." (So that's why my middle name is Denali!) Or, if you believe *Urban Dictionary*, Denali is also known as the "amazing, confident, strong, and smart girl next door who manages to do everything better than you and for some reason puts up with your bullshit even though you're an asshole." Denali also loves dark chocolate and having long conversations. Hey, she sounds like my kind of girl.

If you didn't know, Denali comes from the Native American word for "great one."

The Denali we rebuilt was a 2015 GMC Denali 3500 that a customer brought to us. It was a custom build, so we didn't give it away in a contest. A Denali 3500 is a bad ride and when we were finished with it, it was absolutely sick. We installed a 12-inch Cognito Motorsports lift kit—yeah, you read that right—with upper control arms and a front drop box so the truck would retain its factory drive shaft angles. With 22-inch Hostile wheels and 40-inch Mark Ma Dakar tires, it was a very sweet ride. AMP Research threw on some steps to make it easier for the owners to climb in and out of the cab, and a FASS fuel system and Edge Insight monitor kept it purring like a kitten.

With custom black paint, black grille, black bumpers, and tinted windows, it was a slick-looking truck. We even added a

Decked bed storage drawer system to keep everything straight in the back. While it might not be the most insane build we ever did—who really wants to mess up a Denali?—its simplicity and elegance made it a truck I'll always remember.

That's an important attribute about the trucks we build. Sure, some of them are extreme and unlike anything else you've seen on the road. But even if our trucks are sometimes over-the-top, we still build them to work, whether it's at work or in the mud!

DIESEL HANDBOOK LESSON NO. 8
PROPER MAINTENANCE

Taking care of your diesel truck is kind of like taking care of your body. With the proper care and maintenance, your truck is going to last forever and won't require many costly repairs.

But if you get lazy with regular maintenance, you're probably going to experience some pitfalls and problems and prematurely age your engine. Likewise, if you sit around eating potato chips and cookies all day and don't exercise, you're probably going to have some health problems down the road.

Here are eight important steps to properly maintaining your diesel truck:

1. Change the oil!

If you don't regularly change the oil in a gasoline engine, it's probably not going to last as long as it should. If you don't regularly change the oil in a diesel engine, it's probably going to blow up. Don't be that guy!

The good news about diesel engines is that they don't have spark plugs and don't require ignition tune-ups, which can be rather costly. But it's imperative that you change the engine's oil and oil filter, and you should follow manufacturer recommendations on the frequency.

Also, make sure you use an oil filter that exceeds the OEM filter recommended by the manufacturer to keep corrosive particles from the oil.

2. Rotate and balance the tires.

The key to a smooth ride is getting the wheels and tires to rotate at high speed without vibration, which isn't easy. The weight of the truck has to be distributed evenly on four tires and it can be a challenge—especially when The Muscle is riding in my truck!

Many tire dealers include free lifetime rotation and balancing when you buy new tires. Rotating occurs when the tires are removed and rotated to different spots to ensure they wear evenly, and it should be done every six months or 5,000 or 7,500 miles. Balancing is done to detect vibrations and heavy spots in the tires, which ensures that the tires are spinning around as evenly as possible. It should be done every 3,000 to 6,000 miles.

3. Keep your truck aligned.

If your truck is drifting to one side of the road or you have to lean your steering wheel to one side to drive straight, your wheels might be out of alignment.

Before you take your truck to the shop, check the tire pressure to make sure all four are equally inflated. Underinflated tires can cause a truck to pull to one side, so make sure that's not what's causing the problem. An alignment is going to cost you $60 to $100, and it should be done every year to get the most out of your tires.

4. Check the gaskets.

The gaskets on a diesel engine require regular monitoring because they work under such severe and harsh operating conditions. Check the mounting bolts regularly to detect leaks, which can lead to more serious problems. If you find a leaky gasket, replace them as a complete set. If one is leaking, the others probably aren't far behind.

5. Use diesel treatment.

Every time you stop to fill up the tank (don't pull a Heavy D and fill it with regular gasoline!), make sure you add a bottle of diesel treatment. Over time, diesel fuel injectors accumulate deposits and can become clogged with a sticky, gummy residue. Diesel treatment cleans the injectors and keeps the diesel engine running smoothly.

The telltale sign of dirty injectors is white, blue, or black smoke coming from the engine. If your truck lacks turbo boost or power, idles rough, or is using more fuel than usual, the diesel fuel injectors might be clogged and should be treated with fuel additives. Diesel treatment also lubricates the cylinder walls, pumps, and injectors, which is important in keeping the engine running well.

It's also very important that you regularly change the fuel filter. Diesel fuel injection systems rely on unobstructed fuel flow to keep the pump and injectors cool. If the fuel filter is clogged or obstructed, the flow of fuel is restricted. Make sure to change the fuel filter every 15,000 miles or so, or even sooner if that's what the manufacturer recommends.

6. Change the air filter.

Diesel engines, especially those equipped with turbo, rely heavily on unrestricted airflow to function properly. A clogged air filter causes reduced fuel efficiency and, worse, can also produce severe turbo, valve, and piston damage if dirt gets past the filter. If you're driving off-road in dusty conditions frequently, it's even more important to change the air filter regularly.

7. Wash and wax the truck.

This one is pretty easy, but I can't believe how many filthy trucks I see driving down the road. Take care of your investment and wash and wax your truck regularly. A new paint job and clear coat are going to cost you between $3,000 to $5,000 if the job is done right, and a little elbow grease will go a long way in preserving the paint job. Believe it or not, even bird droppings and diesel can eat through paint, so make sure to wash the truck every few weeks.

8. Inspect the truck.

If you push trucks to the limit like we do, you're probably driving them where most people are afraid to go. But the wear and tear from off-road driving also leaves truck bodies peppered with dings and dents. That can lead to corrosion, which is very expensive to fix if it's not detected early.

Regularly inspect the wheel wells and bumpers of your truck for rust, and examine areas where body components meet because rubbing can cause paint to peel away. Check the door frames, the hood, and other parts of the truck where metal parts meet. Finally, inspect the underbody of the vehicle, which takes the most punishment, especially if you live in parts of the country where salt is used to deice roads during the winter. Make sure to wash the underside of the truck in the early spring, and it's a good idea to mix in a little baking soda with the soap to neutralize road salt.

—Diesel Dave

CHAPTER FIFTEEN
THE FIRST SEASON

HEAVY D: The good thing about having a reality TV show is that you really don't have to change much about what you do. It's just that there are cameras and sound guys following you around everywhere, documenting every single thing that happens in your day. Diesel Dave and I don't have as much time to work on the trucks anymore—we've hired additional mechanics and employees to work on the builds—and our schedules have gotten a lot busier. That's really about the only thing that's changed, other than people recognizing us in the grocery store and airport now.

For each episode of the show, we have to build two trucks. We build and reveal one truck, and then start building another one to keep viewers coming back for the next episode. During our first two seasons, we had to build twenty-seven trucks for eighteen episodes—and they don't give us a lot of time to build them! Each one of the builds is original and it puts a lot of weight on our shoulders to get it done. If we were building cookie-cutter trucks every time, it would be a lot easier, but that's not nearly as cool. It's a lot of hard work, but it's also a lot of fun.

The first two seasons of our show had something for everyone: we went bull riding, built a truck that did somersaults, pulled a locomotive with a truck, and tried to transform a Toyota Prius into a diesel race car. What were we thinking there?

Of course, some builds are more difficult than others, and there were a couple of times we took it right down to the wire to get the trucks finished. Plus, we built sweet rides for some very cool people during our first two seasons. In the second season, former NFL running back Marshawn Lynch asked us to build him a "Beastmode" UTV, which is a heavy-duty all-terrain vehicle, and then legendary actor Chuck Norris had us build him a badass truck for one of his projects, and then he choked out Redbeard until he passed out. We covered Chuck's truck in stars and stripes and named it Truck Norris. We even took steel from Chuck's abs and reinforced the frame with it. (Chuck Norris once peed in a semitruck gas tank as a joke. That truck is now known as Optimus Prime!)

Later in season two, we built a truck for Detroit Tigers star Miguel Cabrera, a two-time American League Most Valuable Player. Miguel's father worked as a mechanic when he was growing up in Venezuela, and he has always enjoyed working on cars and trucks. He asked us to build him a big and powerful truck. He was going to drive it for a while, and then auction it off to help fund his foundations in Detroit and Miami. It was such an honor getting to meet those guys, and we were obviously humbled that they were interested in having us build rides for them.

It wasn't always smooth sailing during our first two seasons. As we were filming the "Full of Bull" episode for season two, we decided to have a dolly race through our garage. For some reason, we thought it would be a great idea to Saran Wrap the Ruth brothers to dollies and put them through an obstacle course. At least that's what we told them we were doing! We were actually setting them up for an epic prank, in which we were going to hook them to a rope and hang them like piñatas for the rest of the day. Diesel Dave also had a pet tarantula he was going to drop on them, since they're both terrified of spiders. Unfortunately, we didn't make it that far. Midway through the race, someone shot me with an airsoft gun, and I accidentally dropped Chet on his head and knocked him out. I ran for the hills, and the other guys had to quickly cut Chet out of the Saran Wrap before he regained consciousness. Needless to say, that's the last time we had a dolly race in the shop.

Like I said, there isn't much that has changed at Sparks Motors.

DIESEL DAVE: The best part of my job is giving trucks away on the show. I like being the guy who picks winners up from the airport or shows up at their front door, hands them the keys to their new trucks, and then takes them out for a steak dinner. There's not a better feeling in the world than giving something special to someone and changing their lives. (Well, I can think of a few things that feel better, but we probably shouldn't talk about it here.) Fortunately, I still get to give away trucks on *Diesel Brothers*.

One of the most memorable experiences I had was when we gave away the Ultimate Hunt Rig in a MTN OPS Truck for a Buck contest in March 2015. We took a 2009 Ford F-250 XLT single cab and put a Sparks Motors custom stackbed on it. Then we wrapped it in a custom Realtree camouflage wrap and added 20-inch wheels with 42-inch Michelin military tires. With a Fusion bumper, custom mesh grille and headache rack, and black bedliner coating, it was the greatest outdoor truck you'd ever seen. If Grizzly Adams had owned a truck, he would have driven the Ultimate Hunt Rig. It was insane, especially with a 6.4-liter Power Stroke engine and automatic transmission.

John Fregia ended up winning the Ultimate Hunt Rig, and when we found out he was from Ennis, Texas, we devised a plan to give him the truck at the National Hot Rod Diesel Association Texas Diesel Nationals in Waxahachie, Texas. We had somebody from the NHRDA call John and tell him he'd won a trip to the races, including free passes and a hotel room. When John called later that week and said he couldn't make it, we were worried. But the NHRDA guys did a great job of persuading him to come.

On April 13, 2014, John and his two young kids rode in our truck during the sled pull. When they were done, I pulled up in the Ultimate Hunt Rig and told him he'd won it. He was so surprised and happy he had a new truck. I guarantee you there's not a better quail rig in the Lone Star State.

One of the more remarkable things about our contests is that we gave away more than twenty trucks in the first three years, but never had a winner from Utah. That shows you how random our contests really are. A third-party company puts names in a big digital hat and pulls out a winner. Like we said earlier, we have a third party select the winner so our contests are totally fair and objective. We have no input in choosing the winner. After the first three years, we had winners from more than a dozen states, including Alaska, Florida, Kentucky, Kansas, Pennsylvania, and South Dakota. But no one from our own state had claimed one of our trucks, even though Utah residents had the third-most entries in our contests. It was beyond time to end the drought. It was time to take care of the homeboys.

When we gave away a 1994 Ford F-350 Dually in February 2016, the guy who won the truck literally lived two miles from our shop. It was the first truck we'd given away after the first season of *Diesel Brothers*. John Mitchell of West Bountiful, Utah, was the winner, and we couldn't have been happier to ride down the road and turn over the keys. John lived in a log-cabin-style home that he affectionately called "Hellhole Ranch." The guy had a ton of character, just like his new truck. He was getting ready to retire and had decided he was going to buy a new truck once he quit working. He didn't have to buy one anymore.

The Ford F-350 we gave him was a rebuilt American classic. We called it OBS 2.0. (If you didn't know, OBS stands for Old Body Style, and the old Ford body style was one of the best.) The truck John won had an old International Harvester IDI diesel engine that had some issues, so we swapped it out for a 5.2-liter, 12-valve Cummins. We also upgraded the transmission with a five-speed manual and dual disc clutch.

The Ford F-350 was a crew cab with a long bed, and the body and frame were still in great shape. It still needed some of our patented upgrades, though. We threw on a Fusion bumper, Monster hook shackles, and a 2008 Super Duty all-black leather interior. We painted the truck white and gray, and the only chrome parts were the 22-inch American Force wheels. The best feature on the truck, in my opinion, was the AccuAir e-Level air management package and Viair management package, which automatically controlled the suspension for a smooth ride. When we were finished, we'd turned the OBS 2.0 into one of the most beautiful trucks we'd ever built.

In the fourth year of contests, we've given away trucks to people from coast to coast. We haven't had a winner from Canada yet, or from many U.S. states that are diesel hotbeds. My advice to *Diesel Brothers* fans who haven't won yet: keep trying. You have to play to win, and my pretty face won't be showing up at your front door if you don't enter.

> You have to play to win, and my pretty face won't be showing up at your front door if you don't enter.

CHAPTER SIXTEEN
#FAILOFTHEYEAR

DIESEL DAVE: Do you know what's better than owning a helicopter, desert racing truck, and badass snowmobiles? When your best friend owns them! Heavy D and I like to spend our weekends riding dirt bikes, UTVs, and snowmobiles, and Utah is the best place in the country to live because we have rocks, mountains, desert, and all kinds of terrain. In the winter, nearby Silver Lake and Deer Creek get a ton of snow, so there's always somewhere to go to have fun.

Not only do we like riding off-road vehicles, but we also love building them. Along with our monster trucks, we've built some pretty sweet UTVs and hunting vehicles in the last few years. Our affinity for UTV builds actually started with a comment from an Instagram hater on August 5, 2015. Since we love throwing Axle Tech MRAP axles on just about anything we build (why wouldn't we?), one of our critics commented, "You guys would put MRAPs on a Civic if given the chance." Well, we didn't have a Honda Civic sitting around the shop, but we did have a wrecked Maverick UTV. A UTV is like a tricked-out four-wheeler; it can go anywhere and do just about anything. So that night, as a joke, we set the crushed Maverick body on top of a pair of MRAP axles.

Almost instantly, the image went viral. People thought we'd lost our minds. There was no way it would work, they told us. In fact, people started a new hashtag—#FAILOFTHEYEAR— and attached it to the photo of our monster UTV. Since we were in the middle of building trucks for the SEMA show and our TV show, we tapped the brakes on fully building the monster UTV, which only made the haters get louder. Critics started leaving comments like, "What happened to the fail? I guess it was the #failoftheyear."

Well, as soon as we had time, we started building the #failoftheyear. Polaris stepped in and gave us a 2016 Turbo XP1000 to use on the platform. Joel Buschmann and his guys at Overkill Racing and Chassis built a custom subframe to bolt directly onto the chassis of the 2016 RZR. The Axle Tech MRAP axles sit under the subframe via four-link suspension, and they're held in place by F-O-A 2½-inch coil-over shocks and hydraulic bump stops. There's a hydraulic pump housed in the subframe that helps turn both the front and rear axles.

Packard Power added a bigger turbo, exhaust, and custom-built drop case that supplied insane power, and GlazzKraft threw in a custom fiberglass body to spruce it up. With 54-inch Mickey Thompson TTC tires, SDR doors, UTV Inc. cage, and PRP bucket seats and harnesses, the #failoftheyear became the #winoftheyear. It was a bad machine that could handle any terrain thrown in its way.

> *The #failoftheyear became the #winoftheyear. It was a bad machine that could handle any terrain thrown in its way.*

In February 2017, we also gave away the HeavyBadger, which was Heavy D's personal Polaris RZR XP 1000 UTV. (I think Ashley finally told him to clean out their garage!) The HeavyBadger was a 2016 model, and we heavily modified it like everything else we build. We replaced the front suspension with a higher-clearance long travel kit from HCR Racing and added 2½-inch coil-over shocks, along with barrel-style heavy-duty tie-rods and Pro Series UTV axles. We added new bucket seats, harnesses, and a cage for comfort and safety, and we even threw on 33-inch Patriot tires. When we were finished, the HeavyBadger was built to go anywhere.

NFL running back Marshawn Lynch loved our UTV builds so much that he reached out to us on Instagram and asked us to build him one. In January 2017, we took a Polaris General 1000 and went beast mode for him. We added a seven-inch lift with 35-inch Patriot tires and 20-inch American Force wheels. We kept the stock engine and transmission, but added a Packard Performance exhaust system to help it breathe easier. The real TLC came on the back end, where we filled the dumping utility bed with four 10-inch Rockford Fosgate subwoofers and four six-inch punch speakers. After throwing in a set of PRP XC bucket seats and painting it gloss black, Marshawn had a sick UTV built for a future Hall of Famer.

One of our sweetest modifications was the Huntin' Fool Camper, which was a stretched six-door, six-wheeled Ford F-650. Instead of a bed, the truck had a camper, and there was "climb-through" access from the cab to the camper. With a 24-valve, 5.9-liter Cummins diesel engine and Ford 5R110 transmission, the Huntin' Fool Camper had enough power to go anywhere. The stock camper was stripped down and reoutfitted, and there's even a removable UTV hauler rack that attaches to the rear of the camper. The coolest part: the camper is powered by one solar panel and a battery setup that can fully power it for seven days. Hunters have everything they need to spend a week in the woods.

While we were building that elaborate off-road camper, we were rerouting the black-water tanks, which are otherwise known as the poop chutes, if you know what I mean. Once we disconnected the old tanks, we filled the toilet with yellow Gatorade and Snickers bars. Then we asked The Muscle to help us align the new tanks from under the truck. When his head was directly under the toilet, we flushed and he was soaked with yellow Gatorade and chocolate bars! If you ever want to experience someone running with the bulls outside of Spain,

I suggest flushing fake urine and feces on The Muscle's head. We've never seen him run so fast!

The MC Hummer, which we bought from Mountain Man, was another fun build. It was a 1998 Hummer H1 soft-top civilian model with a 6.5-liter, V-8 turbo diesel engine. The Hummer H1 is a great military vehicle, but it's also a lot of fun for civilians to drive. It's very well built and dependable, so we didn't have to do a lot to it before we gave it away. We added a Vinyl Wurx flat black vinyl wrap, upgraded the headlights and light bars, and installed a rocking stereo system. Josh Wiles of Madera, California, ended up winning the MC Hummer and claimed a fantastic off-road vehicle.

Not everything we've built that's fun is supposed to be driven off-road. The Reaper, a drag-racing, high-performance diesel truck, is one of my all-time favorites. It started out as a race truck that was already worth $60,000, and then we added another $65,000 in upgrades. With a 6.6-liter Duramax engine with triple HSP turbos, HSP water-to-air intake manifold, 500 percent Exergy injectors, and three 12mm Exergy pumps, the Reaper produces nearly 1,500 horsepower. It's a bad machine and, man, is it fast!

Of course, when we were trying to get the truck ready to race, we tore up the transmission and had to build it again. But our Duramax expert, Chavis Fryer, rebuilt the transmission overnight and had it ready to run a quarter mile in under ten seconds the next day.

When Heavy D decided we needed a bigger tow truck for

the shop, he didn't send us searching for one on Craigslist or eBay. Instead, we found a retired 1992 Spartan fire truck that we converted into a tow truck. With a Detroit 60 series 12.7-liter diesel engine and Allison World 3000–class automatic transmission, the Mean Green Two Machine already had enough power to haul anything. We kept the cab and added a 26-foot roll-back bed with a 20,000-pound hydraulic winch that can recover and tow anything. We painted it lime green and added a custom Sparks Motors grille that makes it visible from anywhere.

Not all of our conversions have worked out. Hey, nobody said we're perfect. In March 2017, we built a truck to race in the Mint 400 in Las Vegas. The Mint 400 is called "the Great American Off-Road Race" for a reason. The 400-mile race through the Nevada desert is the oldest, toughest, and most spectacular off-road race in the country. The only problem: we tried to build and get a truck ready to race in only a week. We worked through the night on the day before the race and had our truck ready for the starting line. But we broke a U-joint on the first jump, and then a bad front main seal knocked us out of the race for good. We went about twelve miles before we couldn't race anymore. It was disappointing, but we didn't expect to be very competitive in our first year. We'll be back with a much better truck in the future.

DIESEL HANDBOOK LESSON NO. 9 TRUCKIN' AWESOME GUIDE TO LIFE

There might not be a magic formula to finding happiness, but I've got an idea of where to begin. No matter how much money you have or how successful you've become, none of it is going to mean anything unless you're happy.

Heavy D and I might have growing companies and a reality TV show, but I was just as happy when I was riding a clunker of a motorcycle through the Amazon rain forest with only a couple of bucks in my pocket. Happiness and health are what matter most, and material things are eventually obsolete.

Here is a list of things to do to find the good life:

1. Buy a diesel truck.

Hey, the first step to finding true happiness is ditching your gasser and buying a diesel truck. I don't care if it's a Cummins, Duramax, or Power Stroke—a diesel is going to completely alter your perception of yourself and everything around you.

Once you turn the key and hear that diesel engine rumble for the first time, you're going to begin to realize what you've been missing. If you ever wondered whether there was more to life, well, you're going to get your answer right then and there.

And jack that sucker up, brother! Your view of the world is much better when it's six or eight inches higher!

2. Grow a beard.

Besides the obvious reasons for growing a beard—it's cool and chicks absolutely dig them—there are practical reasons for having one, too. Think of the money you'll save on razors, shaving cream, and aftershave!

Believe it or not, there are myriad medical reasons for having a beard. Scientific studies have shown that beards protect your face from 95 percent of harmful UV rays. That means fewer blemishes and less skin cancer! And mustaches and beards act as natural filters, keeping pollen, dust, and harmful bacteria out of your mouth and nose.

More than anything, having a beard gives a man tremendous confidence. Growing one makes you feel like you have supernatural powers. Since I grew a beard, I became a better mechanic, driver, husband, golfer, poker player, and cook.

3. Fall in love.

I've always been a bit of a romantic, but I can't tell you how much fuller my life is since I became a husband and father. I'm telling you: you haven't lived until you've loved and been loved.

You can have a garage full of trucks, a cabinet full of guns, and all the other man toys in the world, but if you're not passionate about the relationships in your life, none of it really means anything. Focus on your spouse, kids, family, and friends. In the end, they're the only things that really matter. Make them your priority and your life will be much fuller.

4. Travel the world.

I haven't hit forty yet, and I've been fortunate to travel all over the world. I ran a marathon on the Great Wall of China. I swam with sharks in South Africa. I jumped from a waterfall in Zimbabwe. I rode a motorcycle across Central and South America. That's living, baby, and those are memories I'll carry with me for the rest of my life.

Breaking your everyday routine and experiencing new things is going to bring you such tremendous joy. By traveling to foreign countries, you'll learn about new cultures, try new foods, and meet new people. While you're learning new things, you'll also learn a lot about yourself.

5. Calm down.

We need to calm down and smell the exhaust every once in a while. We're so consumed by our day-to-day lives that we rarely pay attention to what's happening around us. There's more to life—and it's usually right there in front of us. We just have to stop and take notice.

After spending a week in the shop, I can't wait to jump in my truck with my wife and friends and head into the mountains or to the lake. It's like a new adventure every week because I know I'm going to see something I didn't notice before. Open your eyes and take a deep breath. Life is too short.

6. Be tolerant of others.

I love our country, but somehow we've become a nation of gripers over the past several years. It seems like everyone disagrees with everyone else, and there has to be sides to every issue. Hey, let's all calm down, listen to each other's arguments, and accept what others believe. It doesn't matter if someone doesn't agree with you on a certain issue. If somebody wants to drive a Chevy, I'm not going to hold it against him. It's his truck!

Nobody's perfect, and we need to learn to accept other people, with their warts and all. I don't care if you're white, brown, black, blue, or green, you're a human being. I'm not going to be prejudiced toward anyone. Well, except Prius owners!

7. Make somebody laugh.

If you've watched *Diesel Brothers*, you know I like to have fun and absolutely love making other people laugh. It's one of the great joys in my life. If I can make a joke that makes someone have one of those deep, loud belly laughs, it's going to make my day.

Go through life without a filter. Get crazy every once in a while. Tell a joke and pull some practical jokes. You'll be amazed what it does for you and others. People will gravitate toward you, and you'll feel a lot of self-gratitude in making others happy.

8. Wear jorts.

You can have your khaki, chino, seersucker, linen, madras, and cargo shorts. I want to wear jorts, which are really just cutoff jeans. Over the last few years, jorts have gotten a bad rap, and for the life of me I can't understand why. When they're worn correctly—with a T-shirt and cowboy boots—there's very little else that is more fashionable.

Jorts are easily the most rugged shorts made for men, and they're also environmentally friendly because they're re-cycled jeans. You can cut them to any desired length—longer in the fall and winter and shorter in the spring and summer. The next time you're deciding whether to wear khakis or jorts, look in the mirror and ask yourself this: *What would Johnny Cash wear?*

9. Do something nice for someone else.

I told you earlier that one of the greatest joys in my life is see-ing the reactions of the people who win our truck giveaways. I'm telling you, there aren't many feelings that are better.

Caring about others is one of the keys to happiness. You don't have to give away a truck or money; just do something nice for someone you love or even a complete stranger. Cut

your neighbor's grass. Pay for someone's coffee. Leave a big
tip for your waitress. In other words, put a smile on someone's
face. If you want to feel good, you have to do good. That's the
key to a truckin' awesome life!

−Diesel Dave

CHAPTER SEVENTEEN
DIESEL FANS

HEAVY D: It usually doesn't take me long to figure out whether or not someone owns a diesel truck. If they climb in my truck and roll down the window to listen to the engine, they probably own a diesel. If they park their truck in front of our shop and don't look back as they walk away, they probably don't own a diesel. And if my passenger is constantly grabbing the oh-shit handle in my truck, he's probably a gasser. Honestly, I don't have any ill will toward gassers; they just haven't seen the light yet!

I learned a long time ago that money doesn't buy happiness, but it will buy a truck and sweet wheels and tires, and I've never seen a sad person driving a jacked-up diesel. Owning a diesel truck is a way of life, and diesel fans stick together.

Owning a diesel truck is a way of life, and diesel fans stick together.

I'll never forget the time Diesel Dave was driving back to Salt Lake City when one of our trucks broke down in Kansas. He put out an SOS alert on our Facebook page, and immediately our fans responded. A bunch of guys from the Kansas Diesel Group showed up and towed his truck to a shop, where about twenty guys put their heads together and went to work. They rewired the truck and got it running again. That's why I say diesel is better than gas—because owning a diesel truck is like being part of a family.

That's what makes giving away our trucks so special. It's almost like we're extending invitations to people to join our club and way of life, and they become more than our contest winners and fans. They become part of our family and we're connected by our common love of the awesome sound of diesel engines and the infectious smell of diesel fuel.

We've met so many great people through our giveaways, but one of my favorites was Delores McLaren of Pilot Rock, Oregon. She was a mother of four kids (only one boy) and five grandchildren, and she really didn't even know she'd entered our Built Diesel 4 contest. Her sixteen-year-old son used her credit card to buy a few T-shirts off our website, and he casually mentioned to her that she was registered in the contest. She didn't think much about it and went on with her day.

Well, when we tried to inform Delores that she'd won, she was in the middle of a business meeting and kept ignoring our calls. After calling her three or four times, we finally contacted her son, who called her and told her to answer the phone.

Even after we told Delores she'd won, she didn't believe us and thought it was a scam. She kept asking us how much money she had to send to us, or if she had to attend some sort of timeshare seminar. It was hilarious.

Finally, after Delores received ownership paperwork from us, she realized she was indeed the new owner of a 2014 Dodge Ram Cummins 3500. Delores flew to Salt Lake City to pick up her new truck in September 2014. We were happy to learn that she was a truck lady—she already owned a 2011 Ford F-150 and planned to keep both. She operated an assisted living facility, so it felt nice to give a truck to somebody who helps others. It was a bummer for her son because his mom won the truck because he'd used her credit card (you have to be eighteen years old to win anyhow). Maybe she'll let him drive the truck if he does his chores.

Another memorable giveaway winner was Chad Hofer of Bridgewater, South Dakota, who won our Mini Mega Ram-Runner contest. Chad entered the contest by ordering a stocking cap and knife from the dieselpowergear.com website, and then he kind of forgot about it. When we picked his name as the winner on New Year's Eve 2015, he was so excited he woke up his wife, who had already gone to bed. She thought the house was on fire because he was screaming and running up and down the stairs and hallway. Finally, Chad told her, "No! It's a good thing. I won a truck!"

The Mini Mega RamRunner, which is a smaller version of the original Mega RamRunner, is a 2014 Dodge Ram 1500

Laramie. It has a 3.0-liter EcoDiesel engine and an eight-speed automatic transmission. It is a crew cab with a short bed, so it gets better mileage but it's still pretty powerful. We painted it scion cement (it almost looks like a thunderstorm rolling down the street) and added a six-inch lift, RaceMesh grille, EcoTint headlights, custom hood, steps, pre-runner-style fender flares, and 37-inch Patriot tires. It was a badass truck when we were finished.

Kasey Bunch of Katy, Texas, who won a Ford F-650 Super Truck in our Pugs & Diesel Power Gear 650 Truck for a Buck contest in 2015, is another guy who caused quite a commotion when he won a truck. We notified Kasey that he was one of six finalists for the Ford F-650, and then we came up with a very unique way of choosing the winner.

We had six guys, including Diesel Dave and me, sitting in truck chairs, which were placed on top of brake drums. There was a dashboard air bag inside each of the brake drums, and they were randomly wired to a loom. The air bags were detonated one at a time by touching the wires to a car battery. (Warning: Do not try it at home!) The only things absorbing the explosions (and protecting our rears) from the air bags were cardboard and seat cushions. The blasts blew us off the chairs, and Diesel Dave was the last guy standing. He was holding Kasey's name card, so he won the truck. Kasey was watching the live feed at home, and when he won he made so much noise his mother thought someone had broken into the house!

We flew Kasey to Salt Lake City to pick up the 2004 Ford

F-650 XL, but first we had to show off its power. The truck had a 5.9-liter Cummins and a strong Allison transmission. We stretched the frame to make it a six-door cab, and then we added a six-inch lift, Fleece Performance Cheetah turbo, and a leather interior swap from a 2008 Ford Lariat. The F-650 had 20-inch MRAP wheels and 46-inch military tires. With a red and black two-tone custom paint job, it was one of the biggest and baddest conversions we'd ever done.

To give Kasey an idea of the power his new truck possessed, we chained the F-650 to a train—a real, working locomotive engine. We hooked 400,000 pounds to that truck, and to be honest, I had my doubts about whether it could pull the train. But the truck pulled the train easily, and I think it could have pulled one million pounds! Kasey said it was a once-in-a-lifetime chance for someone like him to own a truck like the Ford F-650 Super Truck, and we couldn't have been happier to give it to him.

DIESEL DAVE: I've had the privilege of meeting a lot of cool winners in our contests during the past few years, but I don't think I'll ever forget the time we called Ian Nipper, who was the winner of a Single Cab Cummins in our Built Diesel 6 contest in August 2015.

When The Muscle and I called Ian to let him know that he'd won a rebuilt 2008 Ram 2500 single cab, we pretended like I was making a customer service call. I asked Ian what he'd ordered from our websites, and he told me that he'd purchased a new transmission for his 1998 Cummins, a few T-shirts, and other items. Ian told us that rebuilding the Cummins was his hobby, and he was currently driving a 2007 Honda Ridgeline as his personal vehicle.

After I told Ian he was the winner of the 2008 Ram Cummins, he finally got around to telling me where he was—he was in the labor and delivery room at the hospital with his wife, who was getting ready to deliver their third child! Honestly, I think he was more excited about the truck than his new baby. His wife even jumped on the phone and told us we'd made her husband's day! It was an awesome experience none of us will ever forget. Winning a truck is one thing, but bringing a child into the world is an entirely different blessing. We were so glad we were a part of that day with them.

Another crazy experience was when a twenty-three-year-old kid named Brad Kurtzweil won the Built Diesel 5 contest in 2015. Brad was from Wasilla, Alaska, which is where I went fishing as a kid and where Sarah Palin lived! It was a crazy coincidence. Brad had bought his brothers a couple of sweatshirts off our website, and he ended up being the winner of the contest. He had his choice among four trucks: Chevrolet K2500, Ford F-250 Super Duty, Dodge Ram Laramie, and GMC Sierra 2500.

Brad ended up selecting the 2009 Ford F-250 Super Duty, which was The Muscle's personal vehicle! The Muscle was so depressed about losing his six-door truck that he trimmed his beard and started driving a Toyota Camry. We had to have an intervention (we drove one of our trucks over his car) and talk him off the ledge. The Muscle hated losing a good truck. Brad couldn't get to Salt Lake City for several months because he was tied up with work, so I took Heavy D up to Alaska to meet Brad and see where he lived. We even did a little fishing while we were there. Brad and his dad finally made it to Utah in August 2015, and they had an awesome truck to drive home.

As much as we've enjoyed meeting people like Ian and Brad, I think anybody at our shop would tell you that sixteen-year-old Brendan Brown of Lansing, Michigan, probably had more of an impact on us than anyone. Brendan was diagnosed with chondroblastic osteosarcoma, a rare form of bone cancer, in October 2014. He'd injured his leg while mud wrestling with a friend, and doctors discovered the cancer when his leg wouldn't heal. Initially, doctors removed a portion of Brendan's right leg and inserted a titanium rod to salvage it. But then the cancer returned, and doctors had to amputate his right leg at the hip in July 2015. Two months later, Brendan's father died of a heart attack. Nobody should have to endure that much pain and heartache, especially a kid.

When we met Brendan as part of the Make-A-Wish Foundation, doctors had told him he only had six months to live. Tumors had formed in his lungs and doctors had to remove a portion of his right lung. Brendan kept fighting the disease and never lost his sense of humor; he called himself "Lieutenant

Dan," a reference to the double-amputee character played by the actor Gary Sinise in *Forrest Gump*, after his leg was amputated. Even after Brendan lost his leg, he continued bowling on his high school team. He balanced on his left leg and threw the ball with his right hand. He was still a very good bowler. It was amazing. Before Brendan became sick, he loved riding BMX bikes and dirt bikes and driving his truck in the mud. He was a lot like we were as kids. He loved watching our videos on YouTube and his dream was to drive one of our trucks.

On the day Brendan came to our shop, we let him drive the BroDozer, which was a beat-up Ford F-350 we converted into a massive dune buggy. When Brendan got into the truck, I didn't think he even had the energy to push the pedal down. Somebody told him not to be scared when he climbed behind the wheel. He looked at us and said, "My momma didn't raise me to be a bitch." He cut the BroDozer loose in the mud and had a great time.

We'll never forget his courage and determination to live life to the fullest.

Meeting Brendan was such a cool experience for all of us to be a part of. To be honest, he was probably more of an inspiration to us than we were to him. Sadly, Brendan died on April 4, 2016. We'll never forget his courage and determination to live life to the fullest.

EPILOGUE
THE ROAD AHEAD

OBVIOUSLY, it has been a crazy ride for us during the past few years, and there's no way we could have imagined only a few years ago that we'd have a successful business and popular reality TV show. We have a lot of people to thank for that, including our families, friends, employees, fans, and most important, the Lord Almighty. When you look at what has transpired with us over the past few years, it's hard to imagine the good Lord didn't have his hand in it.

Hey, it wasn't too long ago that we were selling Hyundais and VW Bugs! It's really incredible to see how far we've come. We started as a small garage working out of an outbuilding at another company's yard. We were literally knocking on doors and buying broken-down cars and trucks out of people's backyards, fixing them up, and then flipping them for a few hundred dollars of profit. At the time, it was only two mechanics and us. Now, thanks to a lot of hard work, passion, and the Lord's blessings, we have more than fifty employees working at our three companies.

People ask us all the time if the show has changed us. Sure, we might not have to worry as much about paying our bills or where the money for our next build is going to come from, but that's about it. We still look forward to coming to work every day and spending time with our buddies. We're still having a blast building tricked-out trucks that people like. We're still searching for pranks and stunts that no one else has tried before, and we're going to continue to look for ways to make our trucks bigger, better, and more extreme than before.

We're still searching for pranks and stunts that no one else has tried before, and we're going to continue to look for ways to make our trucks bigger, better, and more extreme than before.

Of course, we know that *Diesel Brothers* won't last forever, and we're thankful that the show has lasted as long as it has. We're mostly thankful that people like you have decided to watch and laugh along with us. When the cameras go away and the bright lights are turned off, we'll continue doing what we've always done: we'll buy trucks, fix them up, and sell them or give them away.

Obviously, building cool and functional diesel trucks is our bread and butter and that's what we'll always do to pay the bills. But if you're going to be a successful company, you have to have fun every once in a while. And we can honestly say that that's our objective when we walk into the shop every day—we want to have a good time, enjoy each other's company, and laugh together. We've met and worked with so many great people, and that is what has really made the experience so remarkable for us.

What's next at *Diesel Brothers*? Only the good Lord knows. One thing is for certain, though: we're going to enjoy the present and get excited about what's ahead. Honestly, when the TV show is over and we're done building trucks, we'll probably get on a sailboat, pull up the anchor, and see where the wind takes us.

Just remember that if you don't know exactly where you're going, any road will get you there, or something like that. Hang on. It's going to be a fun ride.

—Heavy D and Diesel Dave